Dying Modern

Dying Modern

a meditation on elegy

Diana Fuss

Duke University Press

Durham and London

2013

© 2013
Duke University Press
All rights reserved
Printed in the United
States of America on
acid-free paper ∞
Designed by
C. H. Westmoreland
Typeset in Whitman
by Tseng Information
Systems, Inc.

Duke University Press
gratefully acknowledges
the Princeton University
Department of English,
which provided funds
toward the publication
of this book.

Library of Congress
Cataloging-in-Publication Data
Fuss, Diana
Dying modern : a meditation on elegy /
Diana Fuss.
p cm
Includes bibliographical references.
ISBN 978-0-8223-5375-1 (cloth : alk. paper)
ISBN 978-0-8223-5389-8 (pbk. : alk. paper)
1. Elegiac poetry, American—History and
criticism. 2. Elegiac poetry, English—History
and criticism. 3. Poetry, Modern—History and
criticism. 4. Death in literature. I.Title.
PS309.E4F87 2013
811.009′3548—dc23
2013003132

See pages 149–50 (which are considered
an extension of this page) for additional
copyright information.

FOR MY BROTHERS

Jim, who travels abroad

Dave, who nests at home

Dan, who joins me here

AND

Tom, who got there first

Contents

Acknowledgments ix

Introduction 1

1. *Dying . . . Words* 9
   poetry 10
   consolation 12
   defiance 20
   banality 24
   newness 31
   lastness 35

2. *Reviving . . . Corpses* 44
   comic 46
   religious 50
   political 57
   historical 61
   literary 67
   poetic 73

3. *Surviving . . . Lovers* 78
   loving 82
   waiting 86
   leaving 90
   refusing 95
   existing 98
   surviving 102

   Conclusion 107

   Notes 113
   Bibliography 131
   Index 141
   Copyright Acknowledgments 149

Acknowledgments

Of all the intellectual surprises my little book on elegy afforded me, this was the biggest: a book I thought was about dying quietly evolved into a book about surviving. The story of this subtle shift — a nearly imperceptible movement from loss to love — names the very work of elegy, a poetics of loss that does not so much mark the end of love as put a name to love. The arc of this book spans the distance from *dearly beloved* to *my beloved*, a chasm painfully and perilously bridged by the revivifying power of language.

There are many people who helped me travel over this bridge, and still more who were waiting for me at the end. I am lucky to be surrounded by a generous and active community of poetry scholars. James Richardson, Michael Wood, Susan Stewart, Jeff Dolven, Susan Wolfson, Esther Schor, Meredith Martin, and Joshua Kotin are the real thing: poet-critics whose conversation, creativity, and critique humble me every day. I have Vance Smith to thank for the title of this book, *Dying Modern*, which originated as a companion course to his graduate seminar "Dying Medieval." Taylor Eggan and Javier Padilla kindly assisted me with the copyright permissions. My favorite group of interlocutors and conspirators has followed this project from beginning to end: Sharon Marcus, Patricia Crain, Judith Walkowitz, Martha Howell, Margaret Hunt, and Amanda Claybaugh. To James Eatroff, Joanne Fuss, Linda Courtney, Deborah Fuss, and John Newell, I owe my emotional equilibrium and debts that can never be repaid.

It is fitting perhaps that a book on modern elegy has been so generously supported by a grant from the John Simon Guggenheim Memorial Foundation, a fellowship founded in 1922 by two grief-stricken parents in memory of a beloved seventeen-year-old son. Daniel Fuss and RoseMary Fuss know, all too well, the tragedy of losing a son so young. It is to Tom that I dedicate this book, as well as to my other brothers, Jim, Dave, and Dan, who have persuaded me, in a hundred eloquent ways, that it is too soon to give up on consolation.

An earlier version of chapter 1 appeared as "Last Words," ELH 76, no. 4 (Winter 2009): 877–910, and an earlier version of chapter 2 appeared as "Corpse Poem," *Critical Inquiry* 30, no. 1 (Autumn 2003): 1–30.

Introduction

In the early modern period, so the story goes, people loved to talk about death; they relished the opportunity to give the grim reaper his due, commemorating human mortality in ritual, song, and speech. Only in the modern period, historians contend, does talk of death begin to recede. With the post-Enlightenment rise of secularism and waning of religious influence, death became so terrifying that it could no longer be articulated. "When people started fearing death in earnest, they stopped talking about it," Philippe Ariès famously observes of the early nineteenth century, the period in which, for the first time in history, cultural anxieties about death "crossed the threshold into the unspeakable, the inexpressible."[1]

And yet, as the many elegies discussed in this book demonstrate, people did not in fact fall silent in the face of a depersonalized and dehumanized death. Rather they began speaking about the dead in new and increasingly creative ways. Poetry in particular, in response to the social decline of death, concentrated on reviving the dead through the vitalizing properties of speech. At the very moment in history that death merely appears to vanish from the public stage, the dying start manically versifying and the surviving begin loudly memorializing. Even the dead commence chattering away in poetry, as if to give the lie to modernity's premature proclamation of death's demise.

This book explores modern poetry's fascination with premortem and postmortem speech. Focusing primarily on American

Introduction

and British poetry from the past two hundred years, I ponder and probe the literary desire to make death speak in the face of its cultural silencing. What does poetry have to gain by resisting death's decline? Why are words an appropriate vehicle for reviving death? And how do we survive death's reawakening?

To address these questions, I concentrate on three different voices in the poetry of modern death: the dying voice, the reviving voice, and the surviving voice. Each type of elegy showcases poetry's version of a drama queen: the dying diva who relishes a great deathbed scene, the speaking corpse who fancies a good haunting, and the departing lover who loves a dramatic exit. Though by no means uncommon, these literary oddities are so curious, unnerving, or simply unplaceable that each has escaped sustained critical commentary. Dying divas, speaking corpses, and departing lovers all ghost the margins of the traditional elegy, but they remain stubbornly unassimilated, articulating fantasies and fears about death perhaps too protean and unsettling to be explained either by popular conventions of elegy or by traditional theories of mourning.

What draws me to these peculiar poems are not just their extravagant situations but also their eccentric voices: antic, irreverent, incredulous, yet also serious, farsighted, philosophical. They are voices on the edge, situated precariously on one side of loss or the other, anticipating, experiencing, or recalling the painful presence of absence. While some are dramatic monologues in which the speaker is not the poet, many are personal persona poems in which poets imagine their own future selves—lying on their deathbeds, waking in their graves, or coping with their loss. Few persona poems are generically pure, following strict poetic protocol or clear dramatic scripts; these modern exercises in managing loss strike me as especially protean, with shifting perspectives, multiple audiences, and conflicting agendas. Despite their differences, however, dying modern poems have one important thing in common: all choose speech over speechlessness, utterance over

Introduction

silence. Insisting on giving voice to the voiceless, these elegies all imagine death or absence by offering fantastical fictions in lyric form.

Taken together, the voices of the dying, the reviving, and the surviving constitute what I would call a modern *ars moriendi*. This new poetry of the art of dying powerfully testifies to the resilience of certain cultural attitudes toward loss that historians have proclaimed dead in the modern period but that poets have brought vividly back to life. My study of elegy brings to light an intrepid body of poetry that actively resists death's silencing. But it is not, strictly speaking, a work of literary history. Instead, *Dying Modern* is an act of literary criticism, inventing more than recovering a modern *ars moriendi* that comes fully to life through a labor of rhetorical and critical animation. Taking my cue from the poems themselves, I have sought imaginatively to give voice to a voiceless body, naming, organizing, and interpreting groups of poems that undertake the reclamation of loss in the modern period. The book itself is as performative as it is purposeful, perhaps comprising its own distinctive form of elegy.

But while this book is not a literary history, it may well be a literary exhumation, an attempt to revive a literary genre allegedly rendered obsolete by powerful new mediums for resuscitating the dead. Implicitly arguing for the continued cultural relevance of poetry in a multimedia age, this book refuses to give up the ghost of poetic language. In my desire to defend and explain the power of poetry, I stand allied with those scholars who see in the elegy not a moribund genre in historical decline but a vital form in aesthetic transformation.

Perhaps more than any other type of poetry, elegy has been especially well served in recent years by its professional commentators, who together have written books of considerable range and erudition, carefully mapping the classical, historical, political, cultural, and literary evolution of the elegy, from the individual sorrow of Orpheus to the collective grief of 9/11.[2] Teasing out a concern already present to some degree in all these approaches, my own contribution to this growing body of literature explores the ethical dimensions of modern elegy, a set of obligations articulated through the genre's various forms of utterance and address.

Each of my categories of elegy—last words, live corpses, lost loves—stages a fictitious utterance. And each fictitious utterance struggles to offer ethical compensation for the deep wounds and shocking banalities of modern death. At a time when newly discovered narcotics made dying declarations increasingly less likely, deathbed speakers suddenly overpopulate the world of poetic verse, as if to provide the all-important last words that institutionalized death precludes. Poems uttered by speaking corpses also seek to retrieve the dead from the terrifying realities of dying modern by letting their poetic subjects keep on talking right into the grave. Solitary lovers, compelled to separate at dawn, similarly refuse to fall silent, proclaiming their undying love and asserting their lasting grief to anyone willing to listen.

All are consolatory fictions, which may account for why these poems have fallen through the cracks of our current critical paradigms, insisting as we do that grief, if it is truly worthy of the name, has no compensation. Literary critics now tend to read modern elegy as a poetics of melancholia, a despondent and dispirited body of verse that refuses all forms of substitution, transcendence, or redemption: "the modern elegist tends not to achieve but to resist consolation, not to override but to sustain anger, not to heal but to reopen the wounds of loss."[3] The argument carries considerable moral weight: at a time when death has become ever more dehumanized in its technological ferocity, bureaucratic anonymity, and mass ubiquity, compensations like nature, religion, and even art inevitably come up short. Any act of poetic consolation appears highly suspect in an era that no longer knows how to mourn or manage its escalating losses.

And yet I will argue here that, even with the most despairing of modern elegies, we are never, in truth, entirely "beyond conso-

Introduction

lation."[4] What, after all, could be more consoling than the knowledge that there can be no consolation? Melancholia (endless and irresolvable mourning) has become the new consolation, relieving elegists of the burden of finding and providing emotional compensation, either for themselves or for their audience. If the belief that one can ameliorate grief merely by writing a poem is benighted at best and unethical at worst, is turning one's back on the comforting powers of elegy, regardless of how small or great that consolation might be, any more ethical?

The problem is this: while the refusal of consolation may offer the greatest possible gesture of respect to the dead, it also may constitute the greatest possible abdication of responsibility to the living. It is, from the start, a question of audience. Who is an elegy for: the dead or the living? It turns out that what might be ethical for one (the dead) may be unethical for the other (the living). Elegies speak to both audiences, forced to negotiate the impossible ethical demands of a genre that strives neither to disrespect the memory of the dead nor to ignore the needs of the living.

Each of the three traditions of modern elegy I address negotiates this tightrope between the dead and the living, loss and language, in particularly imaginative ways. These premortem and postmortem elegies speak not only *to* the dead but frequently *as* the dead, employing the art of literary ventriloquism to help death be heard once more. To speak not about the dead but in the voice of the dead appears to represent the greatest ethical violence of all, exploiting loss for the poet's own aesthetic gain. And, yet, when modern elegists choose to speak in the voices of deathbed sufferers, conscious corpses, or lost lovers, they risk a more self-directed violence, losing themselves in an abyss of pain that may or may not be their own. Ethics, at its heart, begins in the ability to imagine another's suffering, making elegy one of the most necessary, if perilous, of aesthetic forms.

The ethical burdens of poetic elegy have apparently only increased in the modern period, as elegy's subjects have multiplied to

Introduction

include not just persons but objects, abstractions, institutions, and values.[5] In truth, elegies were always about more than the death of a person; from the Greek *elegia*, for "mournful poem," early songs of lamentation were as much about lost love as lost life. In the dance of eros and thanatos that defines the genre from its inception, elegiac utterances were provoked by the loss of what one desired and the desire for what one lost. Yet it does seem the case that the cataclysmic cultural changes ushered in by modern warfare, technology, and communications have ratcheted up the ethical burden of elegy; poetry now appears accountable to a whole range of losses that appear at least as traumatic as the loss of any individual human life. In no small degree, the ethical task of the modern elegy is to determine what indeed ethics might mean in a world that appears to have lost its ethos, its "principle of human duty."

The ethical challenges facing elegies may well account for their relatively modest length, at least compared to epic verse. *The New Princeton Encyclopedia of Poetry and Poetics* defines the elegy, in the modern sense of the term, as "a short poem, usually formal or ceremonious in tone and diction, occasioned by the death of the person."[6] Because not every elegy is sparse, succinct, or fleeting, the description of elegies as short-lived may refer, more figuratively than literally, to the brevity of the lives they struggle to memorialize. Or perhaps no elegy can ever be long enough to sum up the duration, complexity, and importance of a human life. Elegies, it would seem, inevitably come up short. And yet, as this book will argue, it is by no means a given that modern elegies fail to fulfill their purpose. Elegies do offer their audience *something*, even if this something is, in many respects, precious little. My own immersion into the modern poetry of mourning makes me wonder if we have been perhaps too ready to proclaim language ethically compromised, too quick to dismiss the considerable reparative powers of elegy.

This book is, unapologetically, a meditation on elegy; it is a genre lover's discourse or more accurately an elegy lover's dis-

Introduction

course. I am attracted to elegies precisely because of their investment in reparation, resuscitation, and reclamation, their earnest attempt to buoy the living by holding on to the dead. The literary genre of choice in times of personal and national crisis, elegy taps into the binding energies of both eros and logos to offer up the poetic equivalent of a human life preserver. "Let Love clasp Grief lest both be drowned," Tennyson sorrowfully intones in an elegy for his beloved Arthur Hallam, 133 cantos long and 17 years in the making. Enfolding the dead in its lyrical embrace, *In Memoriam*, a poem of both "calm despair and wild unrest," shows not just how elegy might be ethical but how ethics might be elegiac.[7] In his critical study of ethical mourning, R. Clifton Spargo helpfully notes that ethics and elegy share two important features: both typically view every death as an injustice, and both routinely make themselves vulnerable to the fate of the other.[8] I would go even farther, for in a very real sense ethics *is* elegy: speaking, acting, and surviving in the face of loss, no matter how irretrievable those losses may be.

If the elegies I address in this book are poetic exploitations, they are nonetheless ethical ones, instances of what Barbara Johnson might call "using people." In Johnson's perspicacious thinking, there is a right way and a wrong way to use people. Transferring onto another person represents a right way, a method for assimilating without destroying the other by letting someone else speak through us in an act of identification.[9] Poetic elegy, I would suggest, represents another right way, deploying the powers of figurative language, like prosopopoeia, not merely to recognize the dead but also to bring them back to life. By speaking of love from the place of loss, elegists offer consolatory fictions that are no less powerful for being fictions. Even when elegy's rhetorical arts of resuscitation fail to console, as they often do, poetry is no less worthy, or less ethical, for the endeavor.

Poetry has a responsibility to those who suffer loss. Refusing to relinquish loss, literature's new *ars moriendi* struggles to keep elegy

Introduction

alive, even when there would seem to be no conceivable point for doing so. The ethical wagers of modern elegy may loom largest in the smallest elegy ever written, an exquisitely painful poem by W. S. Merwin:[10]

Who would I show it to

In just six devastating monosyllables, Merwin voices the lament behind every modern mourning poem: Why write an elegy when the beloved is no longer here to read it? Bereft of traditional consolations like belief in eternal life or faith in restorative nature, modern poets appear to speak into a void. And yet this barely spoken utterance is not completely without audience. We are the audience, standing in (no matter how inadequately) for the lost loved one and reestablishing (no matter how tenuously) the broken bond of communication. Elliptical, bitter, disconsolate, Merwin's "Elegy" is also stirring, honest, unembarrassed. A poem that might be taken as the anthem of modern melancholia simultaneously poses the unspoken challenge of our times: Who would I show it to? My meditation on elegy seeks to answer this disquieting question.

1
Dying ... Words

"*Suppose you are on your deathbed,*" the poet C. Day-Lewis ponders in a poem titled "Last Words": "with what definitive sentence will you sum / And end your being?" Betting that the premature deathbed speech is "just the game for a man of words," Day-Lewis's question stands as a provocation, both to himself and to other poets, who find themselves attracted by the idea of authoring a death, even and especially their own.[1] But can any life be summarized and ended in a single definitive sentence? And if not, why are poets repeatedly drawn to the precise moment beyond which language is no longer possible? Pushing voice to its furthest limit, what exactly do poets hope to learn by imagining, and reimagining, the dying hour?

What follows are my first thoughts on last words, inspired by more than two centuries of British and American poems that take as their central subject the dying words or speeches of the unhappily condemned, mortally ill, or piously prepared. Last-word poems can be found in ballads and sonnets, parlor poetry and political poetry, dramatic monologues and poetic dialogues, and elegies and epitaphs. As a group they transcend the formal properties of any one poetic type, sharing instead a single thematic preoccupation: the challenge of dying a linguistically meaningful death. Last words are, at base, a specifically literary problem. Whether written or oral, the question remains the same: What words are the right words for one's final conscious moments?

Chapter One

poetry

Many literary genres are fascinated by the drama of the deathbed and the power of last words. Early nineteenth-century Evangelical revivals produced a host of religious tracts, mourning manuals, published sermons, popular magazines, and fictional works, all of which idealized the power of dying words to ensure a good death and an even happier afterlife. Across a range of genres, deathbed scenes invariably incorporate what the historian Pat Jalland identifies as the central distinguishing features of an Evangelical good death: a slow, painful but fully conscious demise, borne with great fortitude and equanimity by the dying, who, in their final hour, dispense farewells and blessings to attentive family and friends.[2] In a good death, the dying offer proof of salvation through words of contrition, confession, conversion, faith, forgiveness, wisdom, or grace. Informed by three centuries of *ars moriendi* literature, Victorians in particular valued last words for the spiritual, social, and familial functions they could perform: saving one's soul, settling one's affairs, leaving one's legacy, instructing one's heirs, planning one's funeral, and consoling one's family and friends.[3] Yet actual deathbed scenes rarely approximated the idealized version promoted by didactic deathbed literature. Recordings of family deaths, in diaries and letters, suggest that "holy dying" was extremely difficult to achieve in practice, with most private reports of the deathbed recording "bland or banal" last words, if such words are recorded at all.[4] Dying words of any kind are, in fact, hard to find in an age when newly discovered narcotics like morphine, chloroform, and ether made speech itself an unlikely event in one's dying days.

More than any other literary genre, however, poetry played an especially central role in Protestant death chambers, at once promoting the ideal of a good death and compensating for its absence.[5] At the Victorian deathbed, relatives frequently read aloud poems, hymns, or favorite scriptural passages, made readily avail-

Dying . . . Words

able in collections for the sick and suffering. Popular bedside companions compiled for both the dying and their watchers, like Mary Tileston's *Sursum Corda* or Priscilla Maurice's *Prayers for the Sick and Dying*, include entire sections of poems "Suitable to be read to Persons in their Last Hours." These books not only arm the sick with edifying verses on how to die well, they also provide deathbed attendants with exact instructions on how best to read the poems aloud ("very slowly, distinctly, with intervals; not in a whisper or in a loud voice, but clearly and calmly").[6] Because the Evangelical model of a good death required words of uplift, poems were often at the ready to provide meaningful last words when the dying were unable to do so themselves. Consolation poetry was not just a postmortem genre. Its powers of consolation extended to the act of dying itself, providing final words of solace both to watchers and their dying charge when the requirements of a good death threatened to fall distressingly beyond their grasp.

For the British vicar and Oxford Chair of Poetry John Keble, the source of poetry's special powers of consolation lies in its two most distinctive formal properties: rhythm and rhyme. Author of *The Christian Year* (1827), the nineteenth century's most popular volume of poetry, Keble believed that only the controlling power of versification can "regulate and restrain" strong emotions like mourning.[7] While today we tend to view the whole body of Victorian consolation poetry as an extravagant overindulgence of grief, at the time such verse was believed to achieve the very opposite, relieving minds overpowered by strong emotion. "The sigh of poesy steals without startling," explains Lydia Sigourney, nineteenth-century America's most celebrated poet of mourning. Consolation writers on both sides of the Atlantic identified poetry as the most appropriate literary genre for the death chamber, finding versification alone subtle and harmonious enough not to interrupt either the dying or the mourner's "season of solitude."[8]

Of the hundreds of verses that might be readily categorized as last-word poems, roughly half are traditional elegies, commemo-

Chapter One

rating another's memorable or untimely passing, while the other half are self-elegies, memorializing the poet's own future death. Last-word poems thus look either backward or forward, capturing the dual temporality of the deathbed itself, poised on the threshold between two worlds. If poets are repeatedly drawn to the deathbed, and to the scene of love and loss enacted there, it may well be because the promise of an all-seeing "dying eye" conveys precisely the kind of privileged vantage point that poets themselves strive to attain in their writing.[9] Belief in the revelation of life's mysteries on the deathbed as well as faith in the unlimited insight of the dying hour mark poetry's own claim to otherworldly or expanded vision, elevating the deathbed itself to the status of a living poem.

In this chapter I map the richness of an unsung elegiac tradition of last-word poems and simultaneously examine the problem "lastness" poses for poetry. I end my consideration of the dying voice with a discussion of the significance of last words for poetry itself, a literary form fundamentally concerned not only with words that come last but with words that will always last. But first, I survey four main types of last-word poems: the consoling last word, the defiant last word, the banal last word, and the new last word. These many variations on the dying voice suggest that poetry's "last words" comprise a dynamic literary convention evolving in tandem with changing cultural attitudes toward the deathbed. If in the beginning a poet's primary ethical responsibility is to preserve words that may otherwise be lost, in the end a poet's central obligation is to provide words that may never have been left. In either case, last words remain, for minor and major poets alike, emblematic of the very medium of poetry, a genre preoccupied, perhaps more than any other, with the power and finitude of voice.

consolation

As Evangelical literature promoting exemplary Christian deaths began to proliferate in the nineteenth century, so, too, did the poetry of last words. One need look no farther than devotional poetry published by ministers to find last-word poems uncritically perpetuating the fiction of a good death. Henry Ware's "Seasons of Prayer," a favorite consolation poem from *The American Commonplace Book of Poetry* (1831), offers deathbed watchers advice on how prayer might be used to "strengthen the perilous hour":

> Kneel down by the dying sinner's side,
> And pray for his soul for him who died.
> Large drops of anguish are thick on his brow—
> O, what is earth and its pleasures now!
> And what shall assuage his dark despair,
> But the penitent cry of humble prayer?
>
> Kneel down at the couch of departing faith,
> And hear the last words the believer saith.
> He has bidden adieu to his earthly friends;
> There is peace in his eye that upwards bends;
> There is peace in his calm, confiding air;
> For his last thoughts are God's, his last words prayer.[10]

Ware, a leading Unitarian minister, explains to his flock that the watcher's responsibility differs according to the disposition of the dying: with the believer, the watcher receives the prayer and learns by example how to die a good death; with the sinner, the watcher is the one who prays, lessening the sinner's despair by petitioning God on his or her behalf. Last words are not always the province of the dying; they can be shared or even shouldered, taken on by the voice of another in the very act of intercessory prayer so strongly recommended by the *Ars moriendi*.[11]

Last-word poems spoken in the first person operate as a form of ventriloquism, with poets often assuming dying personas in order to imagine their own final moments on earth. Such literary exercises in premature dying may themselves represent attempts to spiritually prepare for death, especially in an age when the faithful were persistently encouraged to imagine their own "perilous hour." These premortem first-person consolation poems, frequently titled "Last Words," routinely adopt the voice of Ware's departing believer, bidding farewell to "earthly friends" as the "eye upwards bends." Thomas Westwood, a minor British poet and a contemporary of Tennyson, imagines as a young man what he might say on his deathbed to his sister, whom he envisions weeping and "watching thro' the long night hours, / By a sick brother's bed":

> Weep not for me! soon, soon the weary one
> Will be at rest, his throbbing pulses stilled,
> His spirit free.—E'en now methinks I hear
> Sounds that are not of earth, the solemn tones
> Of our home's parted band, that seem to call
> Their child away.—Oh! Do not mourn beloved,
> Too long and bitterly when I am gone,
> And doubt not we shall meet in that bright world,
> Beyond the grave.[12]

Westwood's "Last Words" incorporates all the conventions of nineteenth-century consolation literature: a dying hour, a faithful watcher, a prepared speaker, and a promised family reunion in Heaven. The poet's projected last words—"Farewell! farewell!"—echo the simple "adieu!" of Ware's exemplary Christian death. In their sustained focus on not just the dying speaker but his attentive audience, these representative lyrics highlight the most fundamental feature of the last-word poem: its irreducible sociality.

Last-word poems seek to shore up social and familial relations at the very moment of their irrevocable loss. The poet achieves this paradox through a subtle manipulation of audience, doubling the poem's point of address. Helen Vendler has identified two main forms of address in lyric poetry: the horizontal (lyrics addressed to an immediate human audience) and the vertical (lyrics addressed to a distant divine audience).[13] Last-word poems are horizontal and vertical at once. With their final words, the dying console the

Dying... Words

bereaved but always with an eye toward Heaven. Seeking to bridge the seen and the unseen, the poetic rehearsal of last words is conscious from the beginning of its dual audience and purpose: the human audience that must be consoled and the divine audience that must be convinced.

Helen Hunt Jackson's "Last Words" (1881) is a master of the dual audience address. In this commanding speech from the deathbed, written four years before her actual death, Jackson wagers that a gracious final farewell to family and friends may in fact be the best way to prove her soul's sanctity to God:

> Dear hearts, whose love has been so sweet to know,
> That I am looking backward as I go,
> Am lingering while I haste, and in this rain
> Of tears of joy am mingling tears of pain;
> Do not adorn with costly shrub, or tree,
> Or flower, the little grave which shelters me.
> Let the wild wind-sown seeds grow up unharmed,
> And back and forth all summer, unalarmed,
> Let all the tiny, busy creatures creep;
> Let the sweet grass its last year's tangles keep;
> And when, remembering me, you come some day
> And stand there, speak no praise, but only say,
> "How she loved us! 'Twas that which made her dear!"
> Those are the words that I shall joy to hear.[14]

Embedding the vertical address within the horizontal, Jackson looks forward and backward, demonstrating to her audiences both near and far that she is that very sentimentalist embodiment of female virtue: a woman both loving and beloved. If the central condition of dying well is to approach death gladly and willingly, with a pure heart and a clean conscience, then Jackson, by her own testimony, is on the fast track to Heaven.

To modern ears, Jackson's boastful modesty sounds presumptuous, self-satisfied, and not a little controlling. The sonnet's inflexible meter, tightly rhymed couplets, and heavy use of imperatives depict a woman determined to master every detail of her own memorialization, from the tending of her grave to the words spoken over it. Significantly, there are many more last-word consolation poems by women than by men, a gender imbalance that can be attributed not merely to women's socially sanctioned role as ideal mourners but to the freedom the deathbed provides to women to finally speak their minds. The deathbed, historians now recognize, is one of the few areas where a woman's words have not historically been devalued.[15] By artfully assuming the empowered position of a woman on her deathbed, Jackson forbids her mourners from engaging in the traditional elegiac consolations of adorning a grave or praising the dead, and instead she demands from them in death something she may only have dreamt of in life: the fulfillment of her every last wish.[16]

Last words are, in the nineteenth century especially, a powerful platform for many of the socially and politically disenfranchised. In her poem "Last Words of an Indian Chief," Lydia Sigourney adopts a dying voice not her own in order to protest more effectively the massacre of Native Americans:

> Hear my last bidding, friends! Lay not my bones
> Near any white man's bones. Let not his hand
> Touch my clay pillow, nor his hateful voice
> Sing burial hymns for me. Rather than dwell
> In Paradise with him, my soul would choose
> Eternal darkness and the undying worm.
> Ho! heed my words, or else my wandering shade
> Shall haunt ye with its curse![17]

Professing the government's displacement of Native Americans as "one of our greatest national sins," Sigourney narrates the consequences of America's immoral actions by drawing on three related traditions: the romantic literary tradition of the noble savage's power of oratory, the dramatic stage tradition of the red man's curse on the white man, and the religious missionary tradition of the Indian saint's dying speech.[18] To express her strong opposition to the violent appropriation of the unnamed Senecan chief's land, Sigourney ironically finds herself occupying his voice, his thoughts, and indeed his very interiority. Imagining the proud "pagan" chief's indignity at being memorialized by a white burial hymn, Sigourney's lyric ventriloquism paradoxically constitutes precisely such a tribute: a burial hymn like so many others in the Christian tradition, memorializing the noble last words of the martyred dead.

The African American poet Frances Ellen Watkins Harper also turns to the device of the deathbed speech to lend political urgency to the most famous of her many last-word poems, "Bury Me in a Free Land." Part of a larger group of nineteenth-century last-word poems that might be labeled the "bury me/bury me not" tradition, Harper's impassioned call, "bury me in a free land," galvanizes her audience by summoning the considerable moral authority accorded to the deathbed wish.[19]

Make me a grave where'er you will,
In a lowly plain, or a lofty hill,
Make it among earth's humblest graves,
But not in a land where men are slaves.[20]

Unlike Sigourney's political last-word poem, Harper's abolitionist lyric—which rhymes "will" with "hill" and "graves" with "slaves"—works not by concealing an ideological contradiction but by disclosing one. In Shira Wolosky's concise summary, "the land of the free is exposed as the home of slaves, and liberty comes to the dead, not the living."[21] And yet it may be truer to say that even the dead cannot rest easy until slavery has been eradicated. In a slave nation, the poet implies, no one dies a good death.

While Jackson, Sigourney, and Harper all exploit the personal and political potential of last words to command attention and to provoke response, at least one other nineteenth-century consolation poet hesitates to extol or exaggerate at all the power of last words. Unlike her contemporaries, Emily Dickinson uses the deathbed address not to claim agency but to relinquish it. Her well-known "I heard a Fly buzz - when I died" (P, 591) deploys a postmortem voice to question the power of dying speech and to undercut the sentimentalist fiction of the momentous final hour. As speaker and watchers silently await the climactic moment "when the King / Be witnessed - in the Room," they hear only the sound of an "uncertain - stumbling" fly—a grim reminder of the body's imminent decomposition and decay.[22] Strikingly, none of Dickinson's many deathwatch poems include last words. These resolutely discreet poems emphasize instead the radical privacy of death: "No Notice gave She, but a Change - / No Message, but a sigh" (P, 860). Any "changes" recorded by Dickinson's watchers are nearly imperceptible, more gestural than verbal:

> I've seen a Dying Eye
> Run round and round a Room -
> In search of Something - as it seemed -
> Then Cloudier become -
> And then - obscure with Fog -
> And then - be soldered down
> Without disclosing what it be
> 'Twere blessed to have seen -   (P, 648)

Dickinson's dead protect their secrets. Whatever new knowledge the dying obtain at the moment of crossing over is aggressively withheld from the living, who must look elsewhere for signs of the deceased's state of grace.

The longest of Dickinson's deathwatch poems, "The last Night that She lived" (1865), concludes elliptically:

> We waited while She passed -
> It was a narrow time -
> Too jostled were Our Souls to speak
> At length the notice came.

Dying ... Words

> She mentioned, and forgot -
> Then lightly as a Reed
> Bent to the Water, struggled scarce -
> Consented, and was dead -
>
> And We - We placed the hair -
> And drew the Head erect -
> And then an awful leisure was
> Belief to regulate -   (P, 1100)

Speaking from the side of the deathbed, Dickinson's speaker adopts the voice of the communal "we," waiting intently in the company of other watchers for any sign of the dying's spiritual readiness for death. The "notice," when it comes, remains characteristically elusive, no more than a brief mentioning and a quick forgetting. The greatest evidence in the poem of imminent salvation turns out to be the single all-important word "consented," preceded by the poet's own lyrical description of the woman's tranquil demise, depicted as the soft bending of a fragile reed toward water. Yet the poem does not end, as it might, with the actual moment of death but continues to focus on the actions of the mourners, as they gently compose the stiffening body. The final cessation of activity in the room is presented not as the "still hour" described by mourning manuals but as an "awful leisure," afflicting the watchers no less than the corpse.[23] With no more to do, and no definitive last words to temper their grief, these mourners have nothing but faith to fall back on, nothing but "belief" to regulate their despair.

In a Dickinson deathwatch poem, it is the observers who are observed most closely. If consolation is to be had, it is found not in the elusive words of the dying but in the sheer collective force of the poem's powerful communal voice. For Dickinson, it is the poet's job to provide last words, to offer lyrics that compensate readers for the gap between the ideal of holy dying and its all too painful reality. Dickinson's deathbed poems aim to console the bereaved, not for their grief but for their disappointment. Their purpose is to temper expectations of a glorious holy death while redefining what

Chapter One

a good death might be in the first place. Consoling the reader for the ultimate failure of consolation itself, Dickinson intimates that a good death is a modest, mundane, even mute death—the very opposite of a dramatic, scripted, loquacious death, in which salvation or damnation hangs entirely, and often vicariously, upon a fortuitously selected last word.

defiance

The genre of poetry that goes farthest in debunking the fiction of a good death is not the Dickinsonian literary ballad but the more traditional folk ballad. Heir to the English execution broadsides, which depict the dying speeches of often penitent criminals before the gallows, the nineteenth-century folk ballad relies no less heavily on the convention of last words, though these words are typically anything but edifying. In the folk ballad, one finds a roster of characters—thieves, highwaymen, drunkards, cowboys, suicides, jilted lovers—who come to spectacular, violent, and irreligious ends. With its roots in a vernacular oral tradition, the popular ballad speaks to an audience least likely to find themselves in the Evangelical portrait of a peaceful and comfortable middle-class death. Actual deathbeds are few and far between in the ballad's tragic tales, set not in the comfortable confines of house, parlor, and bedroom but in the remote and open spaces of cabin, cornfield, and creek, to paraphrase Louise Pound's apt description. Pound, an early folklorist, collected and published one of the first anthologies of American ballads in 1922.[24] Often reworking the many English, Scottish, and Irish ballads before them, American murder ballads in particular (more than any other type of folklore literature) depend principally on the narrative power of last words to create suspense, surprise, and dramatic resolution. In the American murder ballad, there are few penitent deaths and even fewer distraught mourners. Indeed, more often than not, the mourner may turn out to be the murderer, exposed and condemned by the victim's last words.

Dying . . . Words

In the ballad "Johnny Randall," first recorded in a Colorado railroad camp, a mother poisons one of her sons at breakfast. With his dying breath, the son wills his brother a horse and saddle, his sister a watch and fiddle, and his mother "a twisted hemp rope, for to hang her up high."[25] Upending the pious convention of last words, the fallen son bestows neither love nor forgiveness but death itself upon the murderous mother who betrayed him. Similarly, in "The Cruel Brother" a newly wedded sister, stabbed in the breast by her possessive brother, uses her last words to bequeath "a pair of gallows to hang him on."[26] These grim family romances represent the underside of the *ars moriendi* genre: the capacity of last words not just to exhort and edify but to curse and condemn. Disdaining religious piety, the dying speech in the typical murder ballad constitutes a lethal last testament, abjuring saintly forgiveness in favor of vengeful retribution.

Forgiveness is not entirely absent from the murder ballad. In the well-known nineteenth-century American folk song "The Jealous Lover," a woman violently murdered by her rebuffed lover forgives him in her dying words:

> Down on her knees before him
>   She begged him for her life;
> Deep, deep into her bosom,
>   He plunged the fatal knife,
> "Dear Willie, I'll forgive you,"
>   Was her last dying breath;
> "I never have deceived you,"
>   She closed her eyes in death.[27]

Rose Terry Cooke's poem "Faithful" (1888) features another dying woman refusing to name the man who viciously assaulted her.

> "Nobody hurt me!" They see her die,
>   The same word still on her latest breath,
> With a tranquil smile she tells her lie,
>   And glad goes down to the gates of death.

> Beaten, murdered, but faithful still,
>   Loving above all wrong and woe,
> If she has gone to a world of ill,
>   Where, oh! Saint, shall we others go?
>
> Even, I think, that evil man
>   Has hope of a better life in him,
> When she so loved him her last words ran:
>   "Nobody hurt me! I've saved you, Jim!"[28]

The ballad tradition is replete with women afflicted with what we might call "the Desdemona complex": women who prove their love and fidelity by using their dying words not merely to forgive their abusive or jealous lovers but, more often than not, to exculpate them. And yet even here, in ballads seemingly eager to transcend the violent events they recount by embracing the practice of forgiveness that marks a good death, the faithful woman's *last* last words indict her killer after all. The final line of Cooke's poem, "Nobody hurt me! I've saved you, Jim," points the finger directly at the jealous lover, publicly naming him, if not to the law then to the reader, whose sympathy is entirely for the unfortunate woman, "slain by the man she learned to love, / Beaten, murdered, and flung away."[29] The last words of the Desdemona ballads provide not truth but lies — virtuous lies that offer forgiveness and redemption with the one hand while taking them away with the other.[30]

Ultimately, for all their irreverence, last-word ballads remain themselves ambivalently faithful to the moralizing consolation literature they seek to defy. Ballads like the immensely popular "Wicked Polly," in dramatizing the horrors of an unholy death, endorse, by negative example, the many virtues of its opposite. Too busy frolicking to attend to God, young Polly realizes when she falls mortally ill one morning that it is "too late now to repent." Polly's violent death throes are described in vivid detail: her eyes roll, her face discolors, her nails blacken, her tongue bleeds, and her voice fails, though not before she tells her parents that she is "a lost ruined soul" condemned to "burn forever more." Polly's

Dying . . . Words

lack of spiritual preparation sentences her to eternal damnation: "When I am dead, remember well / Your wicked Polly groans in hell!"[31] No less sermonizing than the conventional consolation poem, this moralizing tale, part of a long tradition of monitory literature, offers its own cautionary lesson on how *not* to die well. Indeed, the poem would parody perfectly the Evangelical deathbed scene, were its tone not so earnest and its language so clichéd. Such poems, in seeking to bring forcefully into view a truly bad death, in the end simply strengthen belief in a good one.

A more successful challenge to the rigid pieties of deathbed dogma comes in the literary satire, for almost as soon as last-word collections appear on the scene, a subgenre of mock last words emerges to check them. In the many eighteenth-century anthologies recounting "last days," "last hours," and "last farewells," readers found confirmation of the final estate of sinners and saints alike.[32] Abandoning simple refusal in favor of canny parody, the satirical ballad responds to the vogue of last-word anthologies by stripping last words of their weighty pretensions and placing them in the mouths of animals. In Robert Burns's "The Death and Dying Words of Poor Mailie, the Author's Only Pet Yowe: An Unco Mournfu' Tale," the poet's ewe delivers a lengthy dying speech from a ditch, where she has fallen entangled by a tether. Advising her master against the use of a leash next time, the ewe charges Burns with the care of her two lambs before blessing her "bairns" with her dying last breath.[33] James Robertson chooses a less innocent lamb for the satirizing of last words in his poem "The last Speech and Dying Words of Willy, a Pet-Lamb, who was executed by the Hands of a common Butcher, for gnawing, tearing, and murdering one of Miss ———— lac'd Ruffles." Parodying the execution broadside, this satirical ballad's "little lambkin" foreswears ruffles, begs forgiveness, and pleads for mercy from his mistress. Finally realizing that he must "atone" for his sins with his life, Willy's loyal "last request" is to be not butchered but turned into lambskin gloves to warm his mistress's hands.[34]

As the specific and symbolically weighted choice of a dying lamb might suggest, these comic satires go further than the more somber murder ballads in challenging the foundational Christian allegory underpinning the convention of last words. In both poems, the shedding of lamb's blood goes unredeemed. Mailie's master, despite the ewe's death, never agrees to stop tethering his lambs, and Willy's mistress, "distant and deaf" to her pet lamb's entreaties for mercy, clearly cares more for her ruined ruffle than for her woolly pet.[35] Moreover, each personified lamb, though closely adhering in its dying declaration to the stock conventions of the *ars moriendi* genre, nevertheless dies less like a holy savior on the cross than a hapless animal on a rotisserie. If these poems never quite achieve the status of blasphemy, it may be because, through their whimsical acts of literary anthropomorphism, they challenge the hubris of even people attempting to die like a god. Insinuating that to die in imitation of Christ is nothing if not presumptuous, the satirical religious ballad might be said to challenge the founding principles of Christian devotional literature no less effectively than the explicitly secular last-word poems that appear more than a century later.

banality

Mock last-word ballads detect the sanctimonious in the saintly, the uproarious in the upright. Undermining the confident assertions of devotional deathbed literature, these late eighteenth-century satires foreshadow what will become a much more serious worry for their twentieth-century counterparts: the unpredictability and utter triteness of the everyday deathbed declaration. Most last-word poems of the twentieth century attribute the poverty of last words to the numbing effects of modern medicine, which offers few the opportunity to "rage, rage against the dying of the light."[36] The poet and critic Sandra Gilbert, herself no stranger to the devastations of modern death, articulates its losses best: "most of the dying do go gentle — or sedated — or anyway barely conscious into death's mysterious 'good night.'"[37] By the end of

Dying... Words

the nineteenth century, death's increasing bureaucratization—its rationalization, depersonalization, and objectification—brings with it a growing recognition that dying speeches may always have been much duller than presumed.[38] In openly confronting the tendency of last words to be hackneyed, tired, unimaginative, unoriginal, or simply unintentional, the banal last-word poem interjects a note of frank, sometimes jaded realism into the history of traditional mortuary verse.

Adrienne Rich, in her poem "The Parting," laments that "last words, tears, most often / come wrapped as the everyday / familiar failure."[39] This everyday familiar failure of last words to live up to their press can be attributed partly to the problem of knowing, even on one's deathbed, exactly when one has entered the fateful hour. "How shall we know it is the last good-by?" asks Louise Chandler Moulton, an American poet and descendent of Calvinists, in the opening octave of her fin-de-siècle sonnet:

> How shall we know it is the last good-by?
>   The skies will not be darkened in that hour,
>   No sudden blight will fall on leaf or flower,
> No single bird will hush its careless cry,
> And you will hold my hands, and smile or sigh
>   Just as before. Perchance the sudden tears
>   In your dear eyes will answer to my fears;
> But there will come no voice of prophecy, —
>
> No voice to whisper, "Now, and not again,
>   Space for last words, last kisses, and last prayer,
> For all the wild, unmitigated pain
>   Of those who, parting, clasp hands with despair:"—
> "Who knows?" we say, but doubt and fear remain,
>   Would any choose to part thus unaware?[40]

The turn into the concluding sestet answers that we can never know it is the last good-bye: "there will come no voice of prophecy, — /

Chapter One

No voice to whisper, 'Now, and not again.'" For Moulton, such uncertainty deprives us of the full significance and experience of last words. The final good-bye can only be truly meaningful if all parties involved understand that there will be no further opportunities for "last words, last kisses, and last prayer." No one, in the poet's own concluding surmise, would "*choose* to part thus unaware."

Or would they? Moulton's question is more than merely rhetorical: "*Would* any choose to part thus unaware?" Presumably some might, and for the first time in the history of the consolation poem, a new possibility has been broached: Are inadvertent or random last words necessarily any less meaningful than prepared or sanctioned ones? Or could it be the other way around: Is it the most devout and familiar last words that have been, all along, the most habitual and "unaware"? In many ways still an earnest consolation lyric, one that places full-hearted faith in the power of "the last good-by," Moulton's traditional poem is also a surprisingly modern one, questioning how much control we truly have over the staging, timing, and content of our final farewells and giving anxious voice to the compelling desire to know (in advance, in the moment, or in retrospect) when any spoken or written words are, in truth, last words.[41]

The problem banality poses for a continuing tradition of *ars moriendi* literature only intensifies in cases of sudden death, when words never intended to be last words are made to shoulder the heavy burden of consolation. In the first major work of her career—an early elegy and last-word poem called "Interim"—Edna St. Vincent Millay adopts the persona of a grief-stricken husband struggling to make sense of the prosaic last words of his wife, who died unexpectedly after scribbling in her diary, "I picked the first sweet-pea today."

> How strange it seems
> That of all words these are the words you chose!
> And yet a simple choice; you did not know
> You would not write again. If you had known—

Dying . . . Words

> But then, it does not matter, — and indeed
> If you had known there was so little time
> You would have dropped your pen and come to me
> And this page would be empty, and some phrase
> Other than this would hold my wonder now.
> Yet, since you could not know, and it befell
> That these are the last words your fingers wrote,
> There is a dignity some might not see
> In this, "I picked the first sweet-pea today."[42]

The grieving speaker at first detects "dignity" in these ordinary dying words, before realizing over the course of the poem that their "trivial expression" is in truth "hideously dignified." Published in 1914, Millay's "Interim," which historically stands at the join between Edwardian faith and modern skepticism, openly rejects the consolations of Christianity or what the poet calls in her blank-verse elegy "that frenzied faith." Secular mourning practices are also found wanting, as the poem's newly bereaved husband refuses to disturb or insult the dead by weeping over his wife, planting flowers on her grave, or conjuring up her ghost. The convention of last words is the one mourning tradition Millay's inconsolable speaker labors to hold onto, though eventually he discovers that he has displaced the meaning of his wife's unassuming last words as surely as he unknowingly discarded the season's first flower that she picked for him:

> 'Twas much like any other flower to me,
> Save that it was the first. I did not know,
> Then, that it was the last. If I had known—
> But then, it does not matter. Strange how few,
> After all's said and done, the things that are
> Of moment.

A last word, like a last love token, may be less a sign from the dead than a consolatory fiction of the living. In the end, Millay's "Interim" discredits the power of last words to tell us anything much at all about life, death, or the proper way to grieve. Refusing to view last words as either the sum of a life or the prediction of an afterlife, Millay presents them instead as simply innocent and inconsequential words, random words whose significance remains difficult, if not impossible, to recuperate.

Twenty-five years after Millay's fictional dramatic monologue, William Carlos Williams publishes an autobiographical poetic dialogue even less sentimental than the despairing "Interim." In "The Last Words of My English Grandmother" (1939), Williams vividly recalls the dreary sadness of his maternal grandmother's deathbed. This de-idealized portrait of dying modern replaces the spare and tidy Victorian sickroom with a dirty and disordered bedroom, less a final resting place than a temporary way station on the now-obligatory trip to the hospital.[43]

> There were some dirty plates
> and a glass of milk
> beside her on a small table
> near the rank, disheveled bed—
>
> Wrinkled and nearly blind
> she lay and snored
> rousing with anger in her tones
> to cry for food,
>
> Gimme something to eat—
> They're starving me—
> I'm all right I won't go
> to the hospital. No, no, no
>
> Give me something to eat
> Let me take you
> to the hospital, I said
> and after you are well
>
> You can do as you please.
> She smiled, Yes

Dying . . . Words

> you do what you please first
> then I can do what I please —
>
> Oh, oh, oh! she cried
> as the ambulance men lifted
> her to the stretcher —
> Is this what you call
>
> making me comfortable?
> By now her mind was clear —
> Oh you think you're smart
> you young people,
>
> she said, but I'll tell you
> you don't know anything.
> Then we started.
> On the way
>
> we passed a long row
> of elms. She looked at them
> awhile out of
> the ambulance window and said,
>
> What are all those
> fuzzy-looking things out there?
> Trees? Well, I'm tired
> of them and rolled her head away.[44]

Last words, Williams insists with this arresting poem, are not always profound; they can be negative, defensive, sarcastic, angry, imperious, and accusatory. They can also be simply ordinary, as the grandmother's weary "I'm tired of them" illustrates. This is not to say, however, that banal last words are devoid of poetic meaning; only that, for a poet like Williams, preoccupied with the immediate, the tangible, and the ordinary, banality is consequential precisely by virtue of its inconsequence. Everything about the poem—from its unrhymed iambic trimeter (which breaks down early and never fully recovers) to its metaphorical invocation of all five senses (rank smell, impaired vision, raised voice, acute hunger, sensitive touch)—aggressively advances the theme of a failing body, dying an embittered death. In a series of tonal shifts offset by the unwavering emotional equilibrium of the poet himself, rage tempers to petulance as the old woman peevishly dismisses the passing trees visible from the ambulance window. Even the actual trees—ordinary American elms rather than the symbolic yews and willows of traditional mortuary verse—testify to the unromantic and unhappy demise of Williams's ill-tempered yet indestructible grandmother, who by the time of her death had already outlived all four of her children.

Importantly, Williams writes two versions of this powerful family elegy. In the first and longer draft, written fifteen years earlier, the poet includes a crucial detail missing from the final poem: a direct reference to his grandmother's dying request for "Mother Eddy's Science and Health."[45] Emily Dickinson Wellcome, it turns out, was a practicing Christian Scientist who did not believe in doctors or modern medicine. Taken to the hospital against her will, Williams's dying grandmother had good reason to be hostile; her grandson, an aspiring doctor, was depriving her of the one thing she desired most—an undisturbed death at home. In choosing to omit this critical piece of information from the poem's final draft, Williams, years after this traumatic family death, may well have sought to absolve himself of guilt and responsibility for ignoring his grandmother's dying wish.

The last words of Williams's grandmother, recorded in a moving ambulance, reflect the new reality of dying modern, in which hospital deaths increasingly replace home deaths and medical professionals become the new custodians of the dying. As numerous historians have noted, in the twentieth century the good death has been replaced by a shameful death—a new type of dying that is as solitary and secretive as the Victorian deathbed was once public and performative. If poetry's banal last words retain deep significance after all, it is by testifying to the banalization of death itself in the modern period. Yet, as the deathbed slowly recedes from view, early twentieth-century poets like Millay and Williams nonetheless choose to hold on to the convention of last words, concluding, in the end, that banal last words are still better than no last words.

newness

Remarkably, as death is driven into hiding and the deathbed virtually disappears from public consciousness, the convention of last words survives into the present, outliving the historical circumstances that produced it. The dying voice proves to be a surprisingly adaptable one, able, through the animating properties of language, to assume voice-altering and shape-shifting form. In twentieth-century poetry, last words endure by becoming gestural last words, humorous last words, or someone else's last words. While the traditional deathbed may have largely disappeared, belief in the power and importance of last words has not. Few it appears, and poets least of all, wish to die "verbally intestate."[46]

More than any other body of contemporary literature, AIDS writing is especially invested in reviving the deathbed and restoring authority to last words. Often estranged from family, concerned over inheritance rights, or anxious about funeral arrangements, gay men on their deathbeds have long turned to the power of last words to wield whatever control they can over an uncertain postmortem future. And yet AIDS poetry rejects the overtly Evangelical conventions of Protestant deathbed literature, striving not merely to secularize the genre but to sanitize it of the preacherly cant that even now tends to judge all AIDS deaths as bad deaths, signs of sinful behavior or moral decrepitude. The single most important feature of an Evangelical good death—spiritual readiness and reconciliation—is exposed, in an age of epidemic, as little more than a tired anachronism.

Chapter One

> And when at last the whole death was assured,
> Drugs having failed, and when you had endured
> Two weeks of an abominable constraint,
> You faced it equally, without complaint,
> Unwhimpering, but not at peace with it.
> You'd lived as if your time was infinite:
> You were not ready and not reconciled.[47]

Nothing, Thom Gunn's "Lament" admonishes, could possibly reconcile one to a death as arbitrary and agonizing as AIDS. The very idea of being "at peace" with such a premature passing is a cruel joke, even a literal one in poems like Greg Johnson's elegy on the death of his friend, Ted Rosen, who with his last ragged breath in a hospital intensive care unit manages to get off a line for the ages: "Many are called, you know, but few are Rosen."[48] Vowing to be memorable if it kills him, Ted Rosen reworks the deathbed exit line into a Borscht Belt punch line, further challenging Protestantism's historical monopoly on last words.

If the original literature on dying well emerged during the late medieval plague years as manuals for those left to manage their final hour alone, then this newer, more secular *ars moriendi* returns the genre to its roots, once again serving as guides for those often dying without the benefit of clergy or family, during history's newest and most lethal pandemic.[49] AIDS poetry revives one of the most important features of the late medieval *Ars moriendi*: its central emphasis not just on the words of the dying but on the offices of the bystander. The very first line of the 1497 *Here begynneth a lytell treatyse called Ars moriendi* counsels its readers that, in the likelihood of death, it is vital to have a "special friend" to aid and pray for you. A historian of the *Ars moriendi* notes that this confusion of audience characterizes nearly all early deathbed manuals: "ostensibly writing to teach a man to die, the author sometimes sounds as if he were teaching a man to help a friend to die."[50]

Nowhere is this truer in contemporary poetry than in the most passionate of Paul Monette's many elegies on the death of his lover

Dying . . . Words

Roger Horwitz, titled "No Goodbyes." Despite a title that appears to refuse the ritual of the final farewell, this poem simply shifts the burden of last words from the dying to the watcher. If modern medicine has deprived the dying of a chance to deliver last words, then it is the friend's responsibility to perform this service in his place.

> at 4 you took the turn WAIT WAIT I AM
> THE SENTRY HERE nothing passes as long as
> I'm where I am we go on death is
> a lonely hole two can leap it or else
> or else there is nothing this man is mine
> he's an ancient Greek like me I do
> all the negotiating while he does battle
> we are war and peace in a single bed[51]

Our deaths are the most singular thing about us, philosophy now tells us; no one can die in our place.[52] Quite so, Monette's poem seems to respond, but like the ancient Greeks one can at least die accompanied, with a sentry keeping guard by one's side. The watcher standing sentry must do what his charge no longer can: deliver the last words that will direct the dying safely across the abyss. As Melissa Zeiger has observed of AIDS poetry, the traditional elegiac distance between mourner and mourned begins to dissolve when the mourner may also be infected.[53] "We are war and peace in a single bed," Monette states, effectively erasing the line between the dying and the living. Writing out of certain knowledge of his own impending mortality, Monette climbs into the actual deathbed to negotiate a truce on Roger's behalf, using the powerful agency of his own dying voice to give final safe passage to his lover.

Contemporary cancer elegies are no less invested in preserving some of the more traditional features of the deathbed, openly embracing many of the observances venerated by Victorian mortuary culture. Two deeply affecting poetry volumes, Douglas Dunn's *Elegies* (1985) and Donald Hall's *Without* (1999), share AIDS poetry's respect not only for the all-important devotional offices of the friend but also for the courageous physical labors of the dying. Recalling the nineteenth-century memorial diary—which recorded, in often excruciating detail, the daily and even hourly activities of the sickroom—both books recount the long illness and last days of a wife dying of cancer. Dunn's poem "Thirteen Steps and the Thirteenth of March" remembers the many "days of grief / Before the grief" when, "like a butler," he served tea, sherry, biscuits, and cake to endless streams of visitors, anxious to pay their respects to his wife, Lesley. Invoking Dickinsonian discretion and decorum, Dunn declines to reveal the content of his wife's final good-byes, electing instead to record their salutary effect on her watchers who, one by one, depart from the deathbed "with their fears of dying amended." "Turning down painkillers for lucidity," Lesley Dunn refuses to be cheated out of her deathbed scene:

> Honesty at all costs. She drew up lists,
> Bequests, gave things away. It tore my heart out.
> Her friends assisted at this tidying
> In a conspiracy of women.[54]

Feeling partly excluded by the authority women have long wielded over the deathbed, Douglas Dunn, like any good Protestant mourner, pronounces his wife's slow wasting a sad but nevertheless "beautiful" death.[55]

Donald Hall's *Without*, an elegy for the poet Jane Kenyon published three years after her death from leukemia, recalls similar deathbed rituals after Kenyon, too, "threw her medicines into the trash." Husband and wife spend their final days together editing a collection of Kenyon's poems, picking hymns for her funeral, and coauthoring and revising her obituary before summoning "the oldest and dearest, to say goodbye." Even more candid than Dunn, Hall records for posterity his wife's last word ("O.K."), last kiss, last look, last spasm, and last smell, as well as his own last gesture—closing the corpse's eyes with his thumb.[56] Literature's newest deathbed poems, like the early deathbed diaries that inspire them,

Dying . . . Words

never hesitate to describe for their audience the physical transformations that they see. In so doing, they bring the most intimate details of bodily death back into public view.

What is new then about the new last-word poems is not so much their bold originality as their subtle familiarity. These poems abjure Ezra Pound's dictum to "make it new" in favor of Robert Lowell's invitation to "tell what happened." As the poet Dana Levin might put it, what is new about the new last-word poems is their refusal to fetishize the new. Writing against contemporary poetry's too ready embrace of the experimental, the first, or the avant-garde, Levin cautions that when we hear the clarion call to "make it new" we should first ask not how but why.[57] AIDS and cancer elegists pose precisely this query, finding in the tradition of consolation literature powerful paradigms for reviving the lost art of the deathbed. As these contemporary elegists show, last words can survive, in somewhat altered form, even in the most hostile of modern environments, including the sterile seclusion of a hospital ICU. By focusing on the physical realities of the deathbed, and by reassigning responsibility for last words from the dying to the living, late twentieth-century elegy keeps an expiring literary tradition alive long enough for the deathbed to finally make a comeback, eventually reclaiming last words as a uniquely shared privilege between mourner and mourned. Like consumption a century before, cancer and AIDS provide the physical conditions necessary for last words; both are gradual and often fatal diseases, in which the dying might remain fully cognizant to the end. Modernity's chronic illness elegies thus announce the latest shift in mortality's cultural landscape, as end-stage patients increasingly choose to forgo consciousness-numbing drugs in order to participate, once again, in the deathbed's most time-honored rites.

lastness

In concluding this investigation of the dying voice in poetry, I would like to give poets themselves the last word. Exactly what are last words to a poet? And why has the poetry of last words lasted? Poetry's abiding interest in last words is partly a function of the capacity of last words to mimic poetry. Like any good poem, last words reflect a heightened awareness of audience, an acute concentration of language, and a profound intensification of meaning. A deathbed declaration, no less than a poetic utterance, draws power from its highly charged investment in a comparatively small number of words. Crafted to have special and lasting significance, last words, like finished poems, command our attention while deflecting our response. The most salient feature of last words might even be said to characterize literature as a whole: with the literal and figurative "death of the author," last words remain unchallenged, inviolate. The power of last words derives precisely from their lastness, from the structural impossibility of dialogue or debate.

But what of the premature last word—the last word that arrives too soon, gets ahead of itself, outlives the moment? Here, too, last words retain their fundamental unanswerability. As the very existence of a robust tradition of last-word poetry might suggest, last words can never come too soon. Dying declarations take preparation, modification, and imagination. As early practitioners of last words knew so well, because we do not know when our death may be upon us, and because we may not be conscious when it happens, last words ideally should be executed in advance.[58] For poets, long invested in Wordsworthian visions of immortality, it is perhaps more important that last words last long than come last.

> Must I be the scribe of each word I speak,
>   never knowing if it will be my last?
> Or should someone else be my full-time scribe
>   (in case deathfits keep me from writing them down)
> Always ready to put ear to my lips
>   in case it should be a whisper?
> "Rosebud." "More weight." "More light."
> "Now it is come." "Now I die." "So this is death?"

Dying . . . Words

> "Thank you." "Farewell!" "Hurrah!" "Boo!"
> "Can this last long?" "It is finished."
> Or like H. G. Wells—"I'm alright. Go away."
> Or like Sam Goldwyn—"I never thought I'd live to see the day."
> Or like John Wolcott when asked if anything could be done for him—
> "Bring back my youth."
>
> I tell myself what my last words will be,
> Hoping I don't get stage fright.
> Hoping I don't get laryngitis.
> Hoping someone will hear them.
> Hoping I'm not interrupted.
> Hoping I don't forget what they are.
> From now on everything I say and write
> Are my last words.[59]

In the final stanzas of this fretful poem, Antler, a former poet laureate of Milwaukee, not only obsesses over his own last words but also wonders how they will stack up against an entire tradition of famous last words, including the most famous last words in literary history, Goethe's "more light."[60] Determined not to miss his death like he missed his birth, this Whitmanesque poet vows to treat all his words as last words. The reasoning is logical enough: if all a poet's words aspire to be last words, then every poem is potentially a deathbed poem, a written guarantee that no poet will ever die without a lasting literary legacy. Rainer Maria Rilke thought much the same, insisting in his eighth elegy that "whatever we do, we are in the posture / of one who is about to depart." Or again, "that is how we live, forever / taking our leave."[61] For these poets, all words are last words because we are never not taking our leave; being itself is defined by our perpetual passing out of it.

Yet how exactly do words last? In a posthumously published poem penned just before her suicide, Anne Sexton depicts last words in naturalistic terms, insisting that words, like ripened fruit, must be artificially preserved: "I have on a mask in order to write my last words / and they are just for you, and I will place them / in the icebox saved for vodka and tomatoes, / and perhaps they will last." Behind her hygienic mask, Sexton fears that, despite all precautions, words can go rancid or stale before they even "reach the icebox / and its hopeful eternity."[62] Picturing how last words might last, Sexton's poetic conceit for literary preservation—the icebox—articulates a powerful temporal contradiction embedded in the very phrase "last words": last words survive precisely because they are frozen, final, spent, quotable, reproducible. It is the chill finality of last words that secures, paradoxically, their enduring afterlife.

Through citation, the dying words of others live on, conferring responsibility and authority on the one who preserves them—a fact that goes a long way toward explaining poets' particular fondness for commemorating the dying words of other poets. Twentieth-century writers as different as Lawrence Durrell, Theodore Roethke, Linda Pastan, and David Ray have all devoted poems to Goethe's dying words, seeing in his cry for "more light!" ("mehr Licht!") an invitation, if not a command, to literary succession: "Friend, you exist, and you lift me up now. / Is that not what Goethe said to the light?" asks David Ray, his very name an embodiment of enlightenment.[63] These poets use the convention of last words to insert themselves into literary history, claiming, as so many elegists do, an inherited mantle of poetic authority.

If last words can never arrive too soon, they also can never arrive too late. Last words are often (if not always) apocryphal words—literary or cultural fictions bequeathed by the living onto the dead. Of the many deceased poets discussed in this chapter, almost none left last words that can be easily authenticated. Deathbed sayings featured in last-word anthologies rarely match up with those recorded in biographies, which may themselves be extravagant exercises in mythmaking, imaginative attempts to make the circumstances of writers' deaths fully consonant with the meaning of their life's work. Lydia Sigourney's widely anthologized last words, "I love everybody," duplicate a dying declaration from Sigourney's own *Margaret and Henrietta*, a biographical sketch published three decades earlier; as Ann Douglas notes, in her final days Sigourney "re-enacted a deathbed scene which she had in part invented."[64] Sigourney's saintly proclamation of universal love does not, however, appear to have been her actual last words; in a postscript to the poet's posthumously published autobiography *Letters of Life*, Sigourney's daughter reports two far less edifying final utterances: "I am so tired, so tired" and "Thank you."[65] Last-word anthologies record two completely different final sayings for Scotland's national poet, Robert Burns, who reportedly exclaimed either "Don't let the awkward squad fire over me" or (in response to a creditor's bill) "That damned rascal!"[66] Neither message though was delivered from Burns's actual deathbed, where the poet, in his final delirium, may have done no more than twice call out his brother Gilbert's name. Contrary to literary mythology, poets' last words are rarely more profound than anyone else's. Sean Day-Lewis, who kept a diary of his father's "oppressive last days," cannot conceal his disappointment when, alone at the deathbed for a final farewell, C. Day-Lewis merely thanks him "for a lovely afternoon," to which his son responds "see you soon."[67]

In cases of a poet's sudden or sensational death, in which inadequate last words or no last words are provided, the temptation to make poetry stand in for inappropriate or absent dying declarations proves too much for most biographers to resist. Edna St. Vincent Millay, who broke her neck in an accidental fall down a staircase, left no last words, which did not deter her biographer from finding them in a notebook the poet was carrying at the time, containing a draft of an elegy for her deceased husband: "I will not flaw perfection with my grief. / Handsome, this day: no matter who has died."[68] More speculation than fact, these artfully selected last lines convey the intended irony: at the moment Millay finally manages to overcome her intense grief for her dead husband, she herself joins him in a post-elegiac afterlife. Sylvia Plath's suicide note, "Please call Dr. Horder," would seem to offer far more genuine last words, a rare instance of a verifiable, indisputable dying message. Yet finding little to inspire in Plath's final instructions, biographers inevitably turn to the first lines of Plath's last poem to summarize her death: "The woman is perfected. / Her dead / Body wears the smile of accomplishment." Judged by one critic to be Plath's "poetic epitaph," the poem "Edge" is considered a more triumphant and eloquent explanation of the poet's purposeful death than the mundane message to call her doctor.[69] Anne Sexton, who left no suicide note, is similarly "perfected" by her poetry, in this case an uncompleted poem called "The Green Room" found later in her purse, or even the entire volume *The Awful Rowing Toward God*, which Sexton had corrected in galley form with Maxine Kumin the afternoon of her death. For biographers attempting to explain a poet's suicide, it appears that there are no more sufficient last words than the poet's own final verses, a position that flies in the face of Sexton's insistence to Plath that "suicide is, after all, the opposite of the poem."[70]

Poets, too, are not averse to dramatizing another writer's last words. Creative citation can give way to outright fabrication in a poem like Tom Clark's "The Last Words of Hart Crane as He Becomes One with the Gulf," which purports to be Crane's final thoughts right before he jumps overboard.[71] Written in the first person and recounting, in broken sonnet form, Crane's own broken spirit and drunken despair, Clark's act of poetic ventriloquism may do no more, in the end, than reveal that a suicide without a suicide note is intolerable to survivors. Last words are intended to be a lifeline, not to the dying but to the living, whose chief means of respecting the dead has always been to quote the dead. Putting words into the dead man's mouth, as Clark freely does, can be viewed as not merely a hostile act but a homicidal one, killing off the dead all over again by refusing to let them speak.

Yet pure citation is not without its own dangers. As Jacques

Dying . . . Words

Derrida cautions in his memorial tribute to Roland Barthes, while an avoidance of quotation simply erases death in a triumph of narcissism, a reliance on quotation merely returns us to death in an excess of fidelity. For the survivor, the poetic stewardship of last words is never uncompromised, even if one somehow manages to avoid the ever-present risks of simplification, totalization, calculation, and appropriation.[72] Given these very real ethical dangers, one is compelled to wonder anew: Why does poetry remain drawn to last words? Perhaps because last words are simply another name for poetry, another way to describe the loss of self, or sense of surrender, which all literary endeavor demands. "When I die, may I be taken in the midst of my work," Ovid once fervently pleaded.[73] Last-word poems reveal that the romantic notion of dying a writer's death, expiring with pen in hand, is for literature a simple redundancy. Writing *is* dying, a way to experience, over and over again, one's own sudden, inexplicable disappearance. As the very phrase "*ars moriendi*" reminds us, Plath was by no means the first poet to suggest that "dying is an art." But is not the inverse also true: Is not art a dying? As the many poems surveyed in this chapter might suggest, *ars moriendi* literature cuts both ways. All literature, and arguably poetry in particular, demands a willingness to disappear into the text, to pass, in Heideggerian fashion, from being out of time.

"Whoever delves into verse dies," Maurice Blanchot bluntly acknowledges in *The Space of Literature*, a book that in many ways reads like an extended commentary on Stéphane Mallarmé's conviction that to be a poet is to be lost in the "abyss" of nothingness. While such a statement may be too totalizing to describe all poetry, or even all mortuary verse, Blanchot's conviction that a poem requires a "voluntary death" does capture, quite precisely, the view of last-word poems that the passion that drives poetry is not the knowledge that the poem will come to an end but the fear that it may never end. The terror of literary confinement happens the moment the poet realizes that to remain any longer inside the poem is to "die in the undertaking."[74] Could the poem be the very opposite of suicide for the simple reason that poetic closure provides a way out? Without closure, no poet would survive the loss of self that a genre like the last-word poem insistently demands.

Mortality, then, is associated not with poetic closure but with poetic composition. Whereas poetic composition denotes an act of dying, poetic closure represents not death but the defiance of death—a running for one's life. Perhaps this is why so many last-word poems, surprisingly, do not end with last words but begin with them. More often than not, poems that memorialize specific last words position them in an epigraph, title, opening line, or first stanza.[75] While some poems, satires especially, are made up entirely of dying speeches, only the last-word ballads, with their strong narrative structure, tend to place last words at the very end of the poem, though even here, they are often contained within a recurrent refrain.

In the twentieth century, the poetry of last words must negotiate the modern preference for anti-closure, poetic endings that favor irresolution and indeterminacy over the conclusiveness and clarity that last words would seem to provide.[76] Of the poets discussed here, only Williams, celebrated in his own time for his "open verse," chooses to close his poem with his grandmother's actual last words ("Well, I'm tired of them"). Invoking the strong closure that only death can promise, this poem comes to rest more securely than most, yet it is a soft landing all the same, as the voice of the mature Williams extends the poem's final line with one more narrative detail, "and rolled her head away." These final words that figure the dying woman's literal withdrawal from the external world also bring the reader firmly back into that world, into the time and space of the here and now, the place of the survivor.

Williams further resists the pull toward teleology by placing the words "last words" in his title, reinforcing the view, prevalent throughout last-word poetry, that the final words of the sick and

Dying . . . Words

dying are valuable, not so much as means to poetic closure than as incitements to poeticize in the first place. If last words tend to gravitate toward the beginning of poems, their early placement suggests that, for poets at least, last words are never the *last* last word. As James Richardson puts it in his second-to-last poetic aphorism from *Interglacial*, "there is no last line we don't have to go beyond."[77]

In the next chapter I explore what this "beyond" might mean for poets who choose to write from the point of view not of the dying but of the already dead. What might the persona of a cadaver communicate that the voice of the dying cannot? When last words have all been spoken, what exactly is left to say? Over the past two centuries, poetry's widening interest in the figure of the speaking corpse effectively turns the lyric convention of last words into next-to-last words. Situated side by side, these two renegade developments in mortuary verse do not so much dispute the idea of poetic closure as defer it, in a world where even the dead are in pursuit of the perfect ending. The increased popularity of speaking corpse poems (which sometimes take the form of postmortem last words) suggests that the most memorable last words may actually be delivered from inside the grave, as writers seek to extend the power of voice into an afterlife of poetry.

2
Reviving...Corpses

"*Corpse poem*" *is a curious paradox.* A dead body and a poetic discourse are mutually incompatible, two formal states each precluding the other. A poem implies subjective depth while a corpse negates interiority. A poem signals presence of voice while a corpse testifies to its absence. A poem quickens language while a corpse stills it. The fantastical coupling of "corpse" and "poem" denotes an extravagant rhetorical conceit, an impossible literary utterance. What to make, then, of an entire tradition of poems that deploy the strange literary device of a speaking corpse? Writers as diverse as Emily Dickinson and Thomas Hardy, Randall Jarrell and Richard Wright, H. D. and Dan Pagis have all used human cadavers as subjects of prosopopoeiac speech. Attributing consciousness and voice to an inanimate body, these writers irretrievably breach the boundary between the place where language intensifies (the poem) and the place where language vanishes (the corpse). Giving voice to the voiceless cadaver, corpse poems bring language more fully in line with death; they are literary fictions that seek to revivify and reauthorize the dead at the risk of contaminating and killing poetry. To give *voice* to a *corpse* changes both.

In its most economical formulation, a corpse poem is a first-person poetic utterance, written in the present or past tense and spoken in the voice of the deceased. At the center of every corpse poem is a speaking cadaver, an insensate figure endowed with the power of speech. By corpse poem I mean poetry not about the dead but spoken by the dead, lyric utterances not from beyond

Reviving . . . Corpses

the grave but from inside it. Abandoning the literary convention of the epitaph, a form of writing that can be read only from outside the tomb, the corpse poem undertakes to bring us inside the tomb, where speech survives the finitude of writing. Leaving no stone unturned, the speaking corpse poem differs in kind from the literary epitaph chiefly in its treatment of voice. While the epitaph reflects what Debra Fried has identified as an awareness "of its divorce from voice, of its condition as a distant trace of a voice now stilled,"[1] the corpse poem betrays a desire to wed itself eternally to voice, a voice capable of surviving death, a voice that conveys not a distant trace but a proximate presence. Corpse poems, in their formal brevity and subject matter, often resemble epitaphs, but not all epitaphs conjure speaking corpses. Put another way, not all poems *on* the tomb are poems *from* the tomb. While some epitaphs translate the voices of the dead, others convey the thoughts of the living. If the overlooked corpse poem has escaped scholarly discussion for so long, this critical neglect may be due, in large part, to the tendency to conflate it with the better-known epitaph.[2]

Corpse poems link the literature of *ars poetica* to the literature of *ars moriendi*, permitting poets to write as if they were in the grave, as if their voices, at least, survived the ravages of mortality. The speaking corpse belongs to that improbable body of literature one might more properly identify as *ars essendi morti*, the art of being dead. *Ars essendi morti* names a powerful oxymoron, since "being dead" annihilates the very possibility of "being" as such. Stretching the limits of ontology beyond the point of reason, the corpse poem poses a series of difficult questions about death, survival, and the animating power of language. Why would a poet wish to experience, prematurely, the state of decomposition, either one's own or someone else's? Why, and when, is a dead voice more appropriate than a live one? What does speaking through the fictional persona of a cadaver allow poets to achieve that writing in their own living voices apparently prohibits? What, in short, is the purpose of a corpse poem?

Chapter Two

In this chapter I explore a variety of reasons for why a poet might elect to speak in the voice of the dead. Again focusing mainly on American and European poetry of the past two hundred years, I examine the cultural functions of the corpse poem in the work of some of its most inventive and dedicated practitioners. Deployed in the nineteenth century principally as a vehicle of comedy or theology, the corpse poem evolved in the twentieth century into a critique of politics, history, or even literature itself. These five registers—the comic, religious, political, historical, and literary—provide the structural scaffolding for my construction of a theory of the dead voice in modern poetry. While I am particularly interested in accounting for the corpse poem's incredible surge in popularity in the modern period, as well as investigating the ethical challenges it poses to the whole genre of elegy, I am also intrigued more generally by the complicated interplay between language and death that this vital new literary form so self-consciously foregrounds. I thus conclude my reading of poetry's speaking corpses by considering the question of why a poem might be considered in the first place a suitable container for a corpse.

comic

In the early nineteenth century, an important shift in the social history of death gives birth to the literary oddity of the speaking corpse. The Enlightenment transformation of the dead body from an object of religious veneration into one of scientific experimentation de-idealizes and de-sacralizes the human cadaver. Industrialism's conversion of the entire corpse into a commercial item that can be bought and sold begins the silencing of death in the modern period. Science's commodification of the cadaver, interestingly enough, did not lessen the fear of death but actually heightened it, creating a new definition of the human body as spiritually irredeemable base matter. Unconsecrated and unredeemed, the corpse crosses into the realm of the unspeakable. But it is one of

Reviving . . . Corpses

the claims of this book that, in this slow, partial, and nearly imperceptible crossing, people were not, in fact, struck dumb by profane and secular death but rather began speaking about the dead in increasingly inventive ways. Cultural attempts to deny death were at once elucidated and counteracted by literature's growing interest in death's diminished presence.[3] In response to the social decline of death and the cultural erasure of the human cadaver, poets began reviving the dead through the vitalizing properties of speech. The corpse poem demonstrates a cultural desire to *make* death speak, inviting the dead to speak for themselves through the poetic fictions of the age. At the very historical moment death merely appears to lose its voice, corpses start to jabber away in poetry, a medium that prior to the nineteenth century had been more interested in speaking *about* or *to* the dead than in speaking *for* or *as* them.[4]

Poetry's earliest challenge to the new cultural reticence toward death is, tellingly, a comic one. Thomas Hood, the first nineteenth-century poet to utilize fully the fictional voice of the corpse, relies on humor to defuse growing concerns over the practice of medical dissection and the industry of grave robbing to which it gave rise. Prior to Britain's Anatomy Act of 1832, resurrectionists stole bodies from graves to fuel the black market in human cadavers, a market generated by increasing demand from anatomists. Several of Hood's poems address the communal fear of corporeal mutilation, gently mocking these anxieties while simultaneously magnifying them. In "Mary's Ghost" (1827), a woman visits her lover's bedroom to complain that body snatchers have plundered her grave, dismembered her body, and sold all her parts for profit:

> The arm that used to take your arm
>   Is took to Dr. Vyse;
> And both my legs are gone to walk
>   The hospital at Guy's.
>
> I vow'd that you should have my hand,
>   But fate gives us denial;

> You'll find it there, at Doctor Bell's,
> > In spirits and a phial.
>
> As for my feet, the little feet
> > You used to call so pretty,
> There's one, I know, in Bedford Row,
> > The t'other's in the city.[5]

This witty poem finds humor in the comic fate of Mary's body parts, with doctors far and wide each purchasing a piece of her. Exploiting the tendency toward objectification inherent in all literary blasons, Hood's anatomical inventory satirizes the commercialization of the body in medical research, a grisly industry that finds economic value in every human part: arms, legs, hands, feet, head, trunk, insides, and even heart.[6] After her corpse has been first "bon'd" and then bartered, all that remains of Mary in the end is her voice. Yet while the presence of Mary's first-person enunciation in the poem might suggest that something human has survived the desecration and dispersal of the corpse, this voice becomes itself a subject of misogynistic satire. No matter how violated, fetishized, or objectified the dead body may become, Hood archly implies, the garrulous female voice will always survive to complain about it.

Hood's plaintive Mary introduces into poetry a tradition of comical corpses who, in bemoaning their fate, merely underscore and reinforce their own cultural irrelevancy. Almost a hundred years after Thomas Hood stages a conversation between a female corpse and the male companion she left behind, Thomas Hardy has one of his many voluble female cadavers conversing with a dog. The speaker of Hardy's corpse poem "Ah, Are You Digging on my Grave?" (1914) finds herself unmissed and unmourned, even by her beloved pet. Hardy's hopeful cadaver learns to her chagrin that the one who disturbs her peace is neither her nearest kin planting flowers nor her devoted enemy defacing the grave, but rather it is her little dog burying a bone—not out of "a dog's fidelity" but simply because he "quite forgot" that this particular spot was his mistress's resting place.[7] Hardy's poem indicates that, by the early twentieth century, cultural anxieties about death have changed from a fear of defilement to a fear of abandonment. Hardy retrieves Hood's speaking corpse to demonstrate how the resurrectionists' illegal exhumations of dead bodies, while disrespectful, nonetheless attributed more value to human cadavers than the modern practice of ignoring them altogether. Possessing not even the impoverished status of a commodity, the cadaver in the twentieth century suffers a fate more serious than exploitation; this body simply disappears, completely buried under layers of cultural indifference.

Most comic corpse poems are cast as ballads, a verse form with particularly strong ties to folklore. The folk ballad, firmly rooted in the popular superstitions of the day, offers an especially suitable vehicle for the articulation of widespread cultural fears about death, bodies, and burial. Long the literary voice of the disenfranchised, the ballad serves as a powerful platform for dramatizing the concerns of the poor, a group disproportionately affected by the medical and commercial trade in human cadavers.[8] At the same time, the ballad form provides a fitting vehicle for comedy, in which the unfolding narrative structure unmasks the helplessness of the baffled corpse, powerless to prevent the dissolution or defilement of a body it no longer controls. Freud's conviction that behind every act of reverence for the deceased one discovers a barely concealed hostility finds independent confirmation in the corpse poem ballads, poems that give voice to the dead only in order gently to mock them. Freud's argument is explicitly historical: modernity, by turning simultaneously away from religious demonology and toward religious piety, diminishes the traditional ambivalence toward the dead, rendering them powerless and slightly comical.[9] Such is the message of the comic corpse poem, where, like "Mary's Ghost," the formerly fearsome dead are literally disarmed by the living. Any residual cultural hostility toward the dead thus takes the form of comedic overkill, reducing an already objectified dead body to the butt of an everlasting joke.

religious

Religious corpse poems also make the most of the ballad, though more for its association with traditional Protestant hymns than for its roots in popular folklore. While comic ballads invoke the speaking cadaver to counter the belief in a sinister afterlife, religious ballads employ the same postmortem point of view to revive the Protestant belief in a benign purgatory, an intermediate state between burial and resurrection in which the corpse is still sentient, neither completely dead nor totally alive. In the nineteenth century, the theological understanding of the status of the corpse hinges on the answer to a long-standing dispute in Christianity over the timing of the Last Judgment. Was the soul judged at the moment of death, passing directly out of the body and out of the grave, or did soul and body occupy the grave together until both were resurrected on Judgment Day?[10] Religious corpse poems investigate the latter possibility, implicitly supporting the notion of a transitional state in which consciousness and voice endow the human cadaver with a distinct presence of its own.

Perhaps no writer has penned more corpse poems than Emily Dickinson, who used the genre to testify to the central tenet of Christianity: namely, that through Christ's death and resurrection, death itself has passed away.[11] Dickinson's corpse poem, "Do People moulder equally" (P, 390), ends with the ironic funeral notice, "Death was dead," the poet's knowing confirmation of John Donne's famous challenge in the Holy Sonnets, "Death thou shalt die."[12] To Dickinson, the death of Death leaves the body of the deceased open to poetic inhabitation. No longer wholly contaminated by death, the speaking corpse becomes more speech than corpse, offering a less threatening vehicle for proclaiming one's faith in the afterlife.

Reviving . . . Corpses

Dickinson's speechifying cadavers, almost always gendered female,[13] are perhaps most memorable for their spirited personalities: gruff, overbearing, peevish, and only occasionally tranquil, philosophical, satisfied. Not easily mistaken for the remote and idealized corpses of Ben Jonson's classical epitaphs, the silent and naturalized corpses of William Wordsworth's romantic elegies, or the ridiculous and macabre corpses of Thomas Hood's popular ballads, Dickinson's female dead are cadavers with serious attitude. "Bring me the sunset in a cup" (P, 140) begins one corpse poem in which the irritable dead, confined to the "little Alban House," demands that her listener compose for her a written catalog of life's treasures:

> Write me how many notes there be
> In the new Robin's extasy
> Among astonished boughs -
> How many trips the Tortoise makes -
> How many cups the Bee partakes,
> The Debauchee of Dews!   (P, 140)

A list of everything the deceased misses most about life, this poem from within the grave expresses more curiosity about what the grave dweller left behind than what awaits her ahead. Another early poem, "Make me a picture of the sun" (P, 239), is no less nostalgic, and no less imperious, as the speaker commands her listener to paint for her a picture of life's vitality to warm her in the grave. Written in the imperative voice of the imperial dead, "Make me a picture of the sun" instructs the painter in the drawing's every detail: "skip - the frost - opon the lea - / And skip the Russet - on the tree - / Let's play those - never come!" Dickinson's dead, homesick for mortality, instruct the living to create for them a fantasy world without russet or frost, a still life without signs of death and decay.

Truth be told, Dickinson's cantankerous cadavers are rarely in a hurry to enter paradise. These displaced dead find themselves exiled from both life and death, at home neither below nor above:

51

Chapter Two

> I never felt at Home - Below -
> And in the Handsome skies
> I shall not feel at Home - I know -
> I dont like Paradise -   (P, 437)

Poised uncertainly on the threshold of eternal life, these anxious corpses express more regret than anticipation: "Eden'll be so lonesome," the dead lament (437). If Dickinson's dead are reluctant finally to "cross over," their hesitancy can be further attributed to their continued preoccupation with the living. Dickinson's cadavers are more haunted than haunting. In speaking corpse poems, it is generally the living who vex the dead, not the dead who unsettle the living. "'Twas just this time, last year, I died," one forlorn corpse reflects, wondering who among her mourners "would miss me least." In her grief at the loss of the living, this corpse consoles herself by looking forward to the time when her loved ones will join her in death:

> But this sort, grieved myself,
> And so, I thought the other way,
> How just this time, some perfect year -
> Themself, should come to me -   (P, 344)

By speaking from the point of view of the usually silent corpse, Dickinson transforms mourning for the dead into mourning for the living. In a Dickinson poem, it is the living who disquiet the dead, the living who disturb any chance the corpse may have for true respite and repose.

Not all Dickinson's speaking corpses are dissatisfied with their lot; a few are perfectly comfortable in their new state of suspended animation. In "The grave my little cottage is" (P, 1784) the speaker happily orders her parlor and lays the marble tea, "'keeping house' for thee," while in "I died for Beauty - but was scarce" (P, 448), two corpses in adjoining graves spiritedly debate the Keatsian question of whether it is better, or worse, to die for beauty or for truth. If Dickinson's contented corpses are unperturbed by their deaths,

Reviving . . . Corpses

their apparent indifference might be attributed to the trait that distinguishes them most: these good-humored speakers are hardly conscious that they are dead in the first place. "I am alive - I guess" (P, 605) presents us with a recently deceased body, a burial bouquet of morning glory in her hands, who convinces herself that, since she is not yet in "a House - / Entitled to myself - precise - / And fitting no one else," she is not a corpse at all but a body twice born. More memorably, "Because I could not stop for Death" (P, 479) narrates retrospectively the speaker's curiously belated recognition that the slow carriage journey that carries her past the three stages of life to "a House that seemed / A Swelling of the Ground" bears her, ultimately, to her final resting place. In these poems Dickinson explores the poet's role as verbal conduit, a voice that bridges "the Distance / Between Ourselves and the Dead" (P, 1068). More specifically for Dickinson, voice carries consciousness, and only consciousness, from one realm to the next. On this point the poet is emphatic: "Consciousness . . . alone / Is traversing the interval" (P, 817).

Other poets deploy the device of the speaking corpse to examine the darker side of the spiritual interval between life and death. Alfred Lord Tennyson's *Maud* (1855–65), a long poetic meditation on love and loss contemporaneous with Dickinson's speaking corpses of the 1860s, and most likely a direct influence upon them, is striking for its complete absence of religious sentiment. Tennyson's self-described "history of a morbid poetic soul" chronicles one man's fall into and out of madness. This poem's speaker, a self-pitying "little Hamlet,"[14] finds himself confined literally to a madhouse where he imagines himself and the other inmates as corpses, buried in a too-shallow grave:

> Dead, long dead,
> Long dead!
> And my heart is a handful of dust,
> And the wheels go over my head,
> And my bones are shaken with pain,

> For into a shallow grave they are thrust,
> Only a yard beneath the street,
> And the hoofs of the horses beat, beat,
> The hoofs of the horses beat,
> Beat into my scalp and my brain,
> With never an end to the stream of passing feet,
> Driving, hurrying, marrying, burying,
> Clamor and rumble, and ringing and clatter;
> And here beneath it is all as bad,
> For I thought the dead had peace, but it is not so.
> To have no peace in the grave, is that not sad?
> But up and down and to and fro,
> Ever about me the dead men go;
> And then to hear a dead man chatter
> Is enough to drive one mad.[15]

For Tennyson's speaker, the intermediate space between life and death already constitutes hell. Delirious and overwrought, Tennyson's speaking corpse provides a vivid contrast to Dickinson's more amiable dead, who even at their most plaintive never approach this degree of despair. His heart a "handful of dust" and his bones "shaken with pain," Tennyson's tortured cadaver cannot escape the incessant noise of the living. Life's "clamor and rumble"—reproduced in the poem through blunt repetition (hoofs, horses, beat), harsh alliteration ("h," "b," and "r"), and frenetic pacing ("Driving, hurrying, marrying, burying")—harass the speaker into madness, doubling his derangement and deepening his disorder. Radically subverting the more serene romantic portraits of corpses slumbering in the grave, Tennyson's *Maud* paints a far bleaker and more cynical picture of the state of the dead, driven crazy by the relentless activity of the living and by the dead's own unquiet insomnia. Tennyson's agonized corpses lie at the opposite end of the spectrum from Dickinson's composed denizens of the grave. While Dickinson places her dead securely inside Death's carriage, as its horses' heads point toward eternity, Tennyson locates his dead di-

Reviving . . . Corpses

rectly beneath the carriage, as its horses' hoofs beat, beat, beat into his scalp and brain.

Writing more in the Tennysonian than in the Dickinsonian mode, Geoffrey Grigson's contemporary corpse poems complete the de-idealization of death begun by his Victorian predecessors. His poem "A Sandy Burial" (1967) confirms Tennyson's complaint that the temporary resting place of the grave is anything but restful:

> "Sucking the dandelion roots—"
> That's a poor milk, you'll agree
> When I sucked a virgin's milk
> And kings knelt to me.
>
> No, I did not "rise again."
> After they buried me
> I lay under the sand here, dry
> As skulls touching the tree.
>
> Big fires in the sky, you say,
> Dry up the sea.
> Act the two-backed pure beast,
> Lovers, on the sand over me.[16]

Cast in the form of a dramatic monologue, in which the corpse converses with a pious interlocutor, Grigson's speaker patiently deflates naïve Christian clichés surrounding the afterlife. This ironic nativity Christ figure, who as an infant sucked a virgin's milk and received the genuflections of kings, does not rise from his sandy grave to ascend into a brilliant fire in the sky but instead remains firmly in the ground, subject to the humiliation of lovers coupling above him. Another short Grigson poem, "Epitaph" (1978), also adopts a tone of stark realism to puncture the idealism that so often cloaks religious representations of the dead:

> They buried me without
> A penny for my fare,

> So how long do I have
> To hang round here
> On this dank gapped
> Wharf under this
> Mud-reflecting sky,
> Watching the polluted
> Stream go by?[17]

Grigson's bitter and blasphemous corpses never cross over to a Dickinsonian paradise. They remain discarded in the dank polluted mud or in the unforgiving sand, pieces of raw sewage or dry bone in a classic modernist wasteland, where there is no promise of resurrection, only the indignity of death itself.

Dickinson's "To die - without the Dying" summarizes the central meaning of the religious corpse poem:

> To die - without the Dying
> And live - without the Life
> This is the hardest Miracle
> Propounded to Belief.   (P, 1027)

This lyric's opening lines precisely capture the main fiction of any corpse poem, a persona poem in which the poet, through the voice of the animated dead, is able "to die - without the Dying / And live - without the Life." To die without the dying is not really death, any more than to live without the life is really living. If a Dickinsonian corpse seems unaware that she has died, it may be that, like the poet who speaks in her voice, she is a consciousness caught between registers, or as Dickinson aptly describes herself, "Myself - the Term between" (P, 743). Ultimately for Dickinson, death is a mere "technicality" (P, 900), a relatively inconsequential event in a world in which to be alive is to be deprived of the eternal life only death can bestow, and to be dead is to be dispossessed of little more than dying itself: "'Tis not that Dying hurts us so - / 'Tis Living - hurts us more" (P, 528).

Reviving . . . Corpses

The corpse poem's chief appeal is thus the opportunity it provides the poet "to die - without the Dying." Yet for the poets who follow Dickinson, this phrase takes on an entirely different meaning, as death's quotidian presence begins to vanish from national consciousness. "The hurry-scurry of modern life leaves no one time to meditate among the tombs," Joseph Jacobs laments in his end of the nineteenth-century polemic "The Dying of Death." Death, he observes, "has lost its terrors."[18] Attempting to recapture a form of dying that has all but disappeared, the corpse poem takes on in the modern period a life of its own. In fact, the corpse poem has never been more popular than it has been in the twentieth century, in large part for its capacity to re-create the intimate particularity of death—from the body's last breath to the corpse's ultimate disposition—that has been so severely attenuated by the rise of the official funeral industry in the late nineteenth century and the trend toward hospitalization in the twentieth century. Modernity, it turns out, is fertile ground for corpses.

political

Most corpse poems of the twentieth century see more gravity than humor in the postmortem lives of the dead. An entire subgenre of modern corpse poems expresses deeply held social commitments, uncovering politics where we may least expect to find it, in the bodies of the dead. Katherine Verdery, in her aptly titled anthropological study *The Political Lives of Dead Bodies*, identifies the two principal properties that make cadavers especially potent political symbols: their capacity to instill awe and respect, and their capacity to instill fear and terror.[19] Political corpse poems dramatize both these forms of identification with the dead, but they do so explicitly to complicate the cultural tendency to treat the dead as either superhuman or subhuman. These corpse poems fall into two general categories: poems that deflate and poems that redeem. The first group humbles those corpses that have been culturally canonized, while the second group elevates those corpses that have been culturally debased. Both kinds of corpse poems aim to correct a social injustice—the politically opportunistic overvaluation of the dead on the one hand and the no less calculated undervaluation of the dead on the other.

Perhaps the most interesting of the deflation poems is Langston Hughes's "Ballads of Lenin" (1938), a political corpse poem that also offers a rare example of a poet ventriloquizing several dead voices in turn. Casting his apparent tribute to socialism in the familiar form of the folk ballad, Hughes, drawn early in his career to Communist Party politics, speaks through the voices of three workers, each addressing Lenin in his tomb with the same refrain: "Move over, Comrade Lenin, / And give me room."[20] The Russian peasant, the black American sharecropper, and the Chinese foundry worker represent in Hughes's poem the voices of the international proletariat, martyrs to the cause whose loyalty inspires the dead Lenin to rise in his tomb and to proclaim the everlasting life of the revolution: "*On guard with the fighters forever! / The world is our room.*" Yet, despite the energetic tone and animated language of the poem, it is conspicuously an army of the dead that Lenin now leads. Lenin's fighting words are no more than that, fighting words; his rousing anthem is a familiar echo, an empty slogan from a movement long buried. As much a critique of revolutionary fervor as an endorsement, Hughes's "Ballads of Lenin" gives vent to the poet's ambivalence about the politics of socialism. By 1938, the year "Ballads of Lenin" was published, Hughes was already subtly questioning the power of dead icons like Lenin to shape the future of the living; a decade later, Hughes would come to view the Communist Party itself as a lifeless movement, an entity as inflexible and distant as Lenin's embalmed body entombed in Moscow's Red Square.

Other political corpse poems use the power of poetic voice to dignify and to honor the dead; these poems inhabit the voice of the dead to make strong moral statements about the cruelty of the living. The poetic device of the speaking corpse has rarely been

Reviving . . . Corpses

deployed to more devastating effect than in Richard Wright's "Between the World and Me" (1963), a poem that details, from the perspective of the victim, a barbarous lynching. Wright begins this long narrative poem in his own voice, recounting his sudden encounter one morning in the woods with what he initially identifies as "the thing":

> There was a design of white bones slumbering forgottenly upon a cushion of ashes.
> . . . .
> A vacant shoe, an empty tie, a ripped shirt, a lonely hat, and a pair of trousers stiff with black blood.
> And upon the trampled grass were buttons, dead matches, butt-ends of cigars and cigarettes, peanut shells, a drained gin-flask, and a whore's lipstick;
> Scattered traces of tar, restless arrays of feathers, and the lingering smell of gasoline.
> And through the morning air the sun poured yellow surprise into the eye sockets of a stony skull. . . .[21]

Recognizing that the victim could have been him, and indeed that the victim *was* him insofar as lynching is an assault upon all black men, Wright finds himself suddenly becoming the "thing" that he describes:

> The dry bones stirred, rattled, lifted, melting themselves into my bones.
> The grey ashes formed flesh firm and black, entering into my flesh.
> The gin-flask passed from mouth to mouth; cigars and cigarettes glowed, the whore smeared the lipstick red upon her lips,
> And a thousand faces swirled around me, clamoring that my life be burned. . . .

An act of unmitigated violence, lynching erases the all-important border between self and world, subject and object, person and thing that separates the human from the nonhuman. By dramatizing in the first person this shift from the human to the nonhuman, from the living to the dead, Wright replicates for the reader the experience of depersonalization and objectification that lynching ruthlessly enacts. Vividly dramatizing the actual lynching—the beating, binding, tarring, feathering, and burning of the black man's body—the poem's climactic stanza is so shattering precisely because the reader's identification with the victim has long since been secured by the poem's subtle shift into the voice of the speaking corpse. "Now I am dry bones," Wright states in conclusion, "and my face a stony skull staring in yellow surprise at the sun."

In spite of its disturbing ending, this poem draws its tremendous power not only from its ability to portray the radical dehumanization of the lynching victim but also from its simultaneous ability to rehumanize the dead through the agency of voice. The lynch mob, the poem's anonymous "they," is never given voice in the poem; the mob is depicted only as a mute and senseless thing, with neither features nor identity. In this poem, all affect and animation reside in the strength of Wright's own voice: shocked, angry, articulate, and, above all, fully present. Turning the tables on the emissaries of violence, Wright portrays the mob itself as a pitiable thing. The lynchers are repeatedly associated in the poem with the detritus of their evening's sick entertainment: loose buttons, dead matches, scrapped cigar and cigarette butts, empty peanut shells, drained flasks, and discarded lipstick. Identified only by their waste products, the mob is more a faceless thing than the fleshless bones of their victim could ever be. Wright specifically chooses the idiom of the corpse poem as a way to bring his readers directly into the horror of the event but also to bring us out of it, through the vital power of his own insistent voice. His adoption of the speaking corpse thus serves two essential purposes: depicting the dehumanization of lynching, in all its literal horror, while at the same time pinning the nonhuman where it decidedly belongs—on the malevolent and amoral perpetrators of racist brutality.

Reviving . . . Corpses

In political killings, the corpse is intended to function as a sign—a message (and most often a warning) to the living. The political corpse poem challenges the cultural tendency to treat the dead body as nothing more than a symbol, an instrument for either the promulgation or the defiance of social change. Political corpses are killed simply to make a point; deprived of subjective voice, these corpses do not so much convey a political message as become the message. The violent reduction of a person to a sign literally kills the messenger, stripping the body that remains of any meaning of its own. By giving voice to the cadaver, political corpse poems belatedly seek to undo this semiotic violence by multiplying the ways in which the dead body might signify and by complicating the terms of both its utterance and its address. These poems ventriloquize corpses not to perpetrate upon the dead another kind of profanation but to make manifest the violence of turning any physical body into a form of political speech.

historical

Richard Wright's "Between the World and Me" illustrates how far the corpse poem has come from Emily Dickinson's cordial and domestic representations of bodies and burials a hundred years earlier. In Wright's starkly graphic poem, the body is mutilated beyond recognition and there is no burial. The corpse has become what Julia Kristeva would call the utmost in abjection: a soulless, raw, and insolent thing.[22] This cultural shift in perspective, from the corpse as the soul's temporary abode to the corpse as pure waste matter, can be attributed to numerous historical factors, including an increased emphasis on sanitation and hygiene and a closer association of corpses with disease. The relocation of cemeteries from towns, and corpses from homes, did not completely erase the dead body from view, but it did fundamentally shift the grounds of its cultural visibility. Whereas familiarity and immediacy provide the common condition of a corpse's visibility in the nineteenth century, anonymity and estrangement increasingly come to constitute a corpse's visibility in the twentieth century.[23] The development of weapons of mass destruction and the emergence of state-sponsored ethnic cleansing take the cultural aggression toward the human body to its horrific extreme, not just dispatching the body but completely destroying it. Technologies of modern warfare and modern genocide render the corpse visible as the thing that can now be made invisible, deploying weapons of such destructive force that the body itself disappears, reduced to a fine grade of dust. "That corpse you planted last year in your garden, / Has it begun to sprout?," T. S. Eliot asks in "The Burial of the Dead" section of *The Waste Land* (1922),[24] the poem's very title a reference to the rotting battlefields of World War I, sown with the degradable remains of bodies too obliterated to be properly recovered and buried.

Given the potential for the wholesale destruction of the body in the modern period, it is at first astonishing to see the corpse poem taking deeper root in a literary landscape one would expect to find hostile to the sentimental Victorian fiction of the speaking corpse. But the historical annihilation of the corpse in the twentieth century does not kill the corpse poem. If anything it revives it, as poets seek to reestablish, ever so tenuously, the sum and substance of being that has been painfully lost. Randall Jarrell's World War II poem "The Death of the Ball Turret Gunner" (1945) keeps the corpse alive by figuratively returning his speaker to the womb to die:

> From my mother's sleep I fell into the State,
> And I hunched in its belly till my wet fur froze.
> Six miles from earth, loosed from its dream of life,
> I woke to black flak and the nightmare fighters.
> When I died they washed me out of the turret with a hose.[25]

This speaker dies before he is born, killed by enemy machine-gun fire in the belly of an American bomber. Playing on the visual re-

Reviving . . . Corpses

semblance of a man hunched upside down in a ball turret to a fetus curled in the womb, Jarrell employs the impossible voice of the aborted unborn to convey the full horror of the gunner's premature death, a death that evacuates the speaker from a body he has barely begun to inhabit. Like the corpse poems that precede it, this body that vanishes leaves a voice behind, a voice that recounts to the living the mysteries of dying. Jarrell's postmortem voice, however, differs from the others I have addressed so far; his is a strikingly distant and dispassionate voice, more laconic than descriptive, more empty than emotional. The voice that brings the speaker momentarily back to life for the reader is decidedly a dead voice, a voice denuded of particularity and distinction.

Jarrell's longer war poem "Losses" (1945) helps to explain the peculiar flat tones of his speaking dead. If his speakers are largely devoid of the animation that death ordinarily and ironically brings to the personas of corpse poems, it is because Jarrell's unburied dead have been denied the liberty of actually dying, an event that is as much rhetorical as it is physical. "Losses" begins with a close paraphrase of Dickinson's "To die - without the Dying":

> It was not dying: everybody died.
> It was not dying: we had died before
> In the routine crashes—and our fields
> Called up the papers, wrote home to our folks,
> And the rates rose, all because of us.[26]

In an age of mass death and world war, Jarrell's dead bemoan what Dickinson's dead celebrate: the death of dying. The soldiers of World War II are not individuals who have died but are mere numbers on an ever-rising mortality index. Sucked out of bombers or scattered on mountains, these soldiers' violent deaths are barely recognized as such. No tombs, no monuments, no wakes or funerals mark their passing; instead, the war dead receive only the courtesy of a death notice sent home. It is the euphemistic rhetoric and sterile politics of modern warfare, Jarrell contends, that has

Chapter Two

cheated these soldiers of their deaths: "When we died they said, 'Our casualties were low.'" Casualties rather than corpses, the dead lose their individuality. Jarrell chooses to speak in the first-person plural "we" for nearly the entire poem to underscore the deep depersonalization of modern death for any soldier. Only at the end of the poem does the first-person singular pronoun make a triple appearance in a tentative assertion that the speaker is, in fact, dead: "the night I died I dreamed that I was dead." This solitary voice laboring to emerge from under the weight of the poem's collective pronoun confirms that, in the final analysis, the greatest of wartime "losses" is the loss of one's right to die as an "I" and not a "we," the loss of one's personal, private, and singular death.

While corpse poems can be found throughout twentieth-century literature, especially in the poetry of the two world wars, there is one group of modern poems in which the genre is notably less common. Only occasionally does one find a poet of the Holocaust inhabiting the voice of a speaking cadaver; the Holocaust appears to mark the historical limit beyond which the corpse poem hesitates to venture. The point is clear: after the unthinkable event of genocide, no fiction of the living dead can possibly be sustained. For poets like Paul Celan or Tadeusz Borowski, death really has died, and mere words cannot bring it back. In the poems of these two death camp survivors, resurrection is a lost hope, and the speaking corpse an indecorous and cruel fantasy. "The dead will not rise from common graves / and brittle ash won't come back to life," Borowski admonishes in his anti-elegy "Farewell to Maria" (1942). Belief in personal resurrection has altogether faded, "burned away in the flames of the crematorium." Celan is similarly blunt in his ironically titled "Psalm" (1963): "No one kneads us again out of earth and clay, / no one incants our dust. / No one."[27] Not even the lyric's traditional theme of dying, it appears, can furnish sufficient "inspiration to poets creating verbal tombs for a murdered people."[28]

The few Holocaust poets who do employ the voice of the dead tend to adopt neither an individual nor a collective persona but a

Reviving . . . Corpses

unique voice that is both at once. "'I am I' — / thousands of slaughtered I's," Jacob Glatstein declares in a poem that reveals not the poet's desire to revive the dead but rather his own profound identification with the dead.[29] Recent trauma theory reminds us that one might survive an unthinkable atrocity like the Holocaust and yet still not feel alive, a point made particularly eloquently by Charlotte Delbo in *Auschwitz and After*: "I died in Auschwitz, but no one knows it."[30] The device of the speaking corpse articulates the sense among many Holocaust surviving poets that they have already died and that their poetic tributes to the dead include themselves.

> And I myself
> am one massive, soundless scream
> above the thousand thousand buried here.
> I am
>   each old man
>   here shot dead.
> I am
>   every child
>   here shot dead.
> Nothing in me
>   shall ever forget![31]

These lines by Yevgeny Yevtushenko commemorate the thirty-three thousand Soviet Jews executed in the ravine at Babii Yar. With no monument to solemnize the site, the poet offers a silent scream, the poem itself, as a grim memorial to Babii Yar's "thousands of slaughtered I's." Both Glatstein's and Yevtushenko's poetic "I's" function, in effect, as communal "we's." Allowing the dead to speak through them, each poet tentatively seeks to reverse the depersonalization of mass murder by lending to the unmourned victims of genocide his own individual voice. These singular poems do not presume to resurrect the dead, only to memorialize them from the respectful position of writers confronting the enigma of their own uncertain survivals.

The experience of being alive yet already dead or, more accu-

Chapter Two

rately, of having died before one's death, introduces into poetry a whole new verb tense: the past participle of modern genocide. Consider these lines from Dan Pagis's "An Opening to Satan":

> As he waited in front of the new invention,
> Danton said, "The verb *to guillotine*
> (this brand-new verb of ours) is limited
> in the tenses and persons of its conjugation:
> for example, I shall not have a chance to say
> *I was guillotined."*
>
> Acute and poignant, that sentence, but naive.
> Here am I (and I'm nobody special),
> I was beheaded
> I was hanged
> I was burned
> I was shot
> I was massacred.
> I was forgotten.[32]

Written in the wake of Pagis's three-year incarceration in a Ukrainian concentration camp, "An Opening to Satan" conjugates, with resolute precision, the number and tense of state-sanctioned executions. Danton's wry declaration during the French Revolution that his imminent death by guillotine precludes the statement "I was guillotined" is contradicted by the twentieth century's newer and more efficient technologies of death, so fearsome in purpose and comprehensive in reach that even those who have escaped destruction feel singed by their power. For a survivor of mass murder, the statements "I was beheaded, hanged, burned, shot, massacred, and forgotten" hold psychological and moral truth, and nowhere more so than when that survivor assumes the grave responsibility of speaking for all the slain, as Pagis does in several of his most important poems.[33]

Historical corpse poems offset the cultural process of forgetting

Reviving . . . Corpses

with the literary work of remembering. Recognizing the power of the corpse itself to keep historical memory alive, these poems remind us that even the most abject body has a story to tell. A corpse is never completely silent, for, as any forensic pathologist knows, its materiality speaks volumes about the circumstances of its passing, the when, where, and how of its demise. A historical corpse poem puts these stories into words, inventing paradoxical new grammars to articulate the terrifying new realities of modern death.

literary

In the range of corpse poems this chapter has addressed so far, figures of speech come to stand in for the missing or forgotten corpses of history. Yet events like the lynching of African Americans or the massacre of European Jewry cannot be comfortably contained in any poem, including the unconventional corpse poem. Language can, at best, only imperfectly fill the void the absent corpse has left behind. If the modern corpse poem partially succeeds in addressing such difficult topics where traditional elegy fails, it may be because the fiction of the speaking corpse allows survivors of traumatic events to express their own feelings of premature death without either sentimentalizing or objectifying the dead with whom they identify. In the end, the corpse poem contests the aims of traditional mourning poetry by dismissing both compensation and its refusal, the twin lures of literary elegy.

To be sure, the modern corpse poem shares many features with the elegy, including both a concern with the certitude of death and a faith in the reanimating powers of language. But unlike the elegy, the corpse poem rarely presumes to console the living for losses so profound that they transcend the compensations of mourning. The corpse poem rejects the elegy's poetics of apostrophe, a rhetorical trope that, in addressing the dead, inevitably draws attention back to the living. Apostrophe, in maintaining a clear distance between the living and the dead, between the "I" who speaks and the "you" who remains silent, operates as simply another more subtle means of obscuring the dead.[34] Through the rhetorical animation of the dead made possible by the trope of prosopopoeia, the corpse poem seeks instead to redress the historical erasure of the corpse that even literary criticism has at times promoted. Dismissed by Wordsworth as a "tender fiction," prosopopoeia falls out of critical favor in the early nineteenth century, only to be reanimated in the late twentieth century by Paul de Man, who resuscitates prosopopoeia as "the master trope of poetic discourse."[35] When prosopopoeia is allowed to speak freely, it speaks loudly, claiming to be the figure for figurality itself, the very voice of poetry.[36]

Deconstruction's retrieval of prosopopoeia at the end of the twentieth century helps bring the corpse poem to light, providing a historical opening for the critical assessment of a genre long concealed behind the more popular elegy. The ambition of the literary corpse poem—which often incorporates elements of the comic, religious, political, or historical corpse poem—is in fact to provide a counter or corrective to the ageing elegy. John Payne's sonnet "Resurrection" (1920), an ironic religious corpse poem in which the speaker rebels against returning to a world he perceives as full of "vengeance and wrath and sorrow's bitter brunt," subtly deflates the elegy's conventional tribute to the day of Resurrection:

> The trumpet calls; the graves gape open wide;
> The shrilling clangours rend the shivering skies;
> The sheeted dead sit up and rub their eyes,
> It seems but yesterday since I, I died.[37]

Payne's weary speaker has no desire to heed the trumpet call and to rise from the grave to meet his maker. Come the day of reckoning, this slumbering corpse intends to roll over and to go back to bed: "Rise who may, / I will sleep on and let God pass away." The dead, Payne suggests, prefer to be left alone, undisturbed by man, by trumpets, and by God himself. Payne's exhausted and jaded

Reviving . . . Corpses

corpse revives only long enough in this fourteen-line poem to repudiate the elegy's chief consolatory fiction: the desirability of a conscious afterlife.

Most modern corpses prefer inhabiting the way station of the grave to the unhappy alternatives of either entering what Dickinson calls the eternal recess of a life ever after (P, 413) or returning to the endless labors of a life already lived. Roy Fuller's "Ghost Voice" (1980)—an especially apt title for describing the spectral utterances of any corpse poem—openly celebrates the freedom of the dead from life's dual burdens of duty and concern:

> The greatest sacrifice
> Giving up the everyday.
> But now I almost enjoy
> This liberty bizarre:
> Responsibilities gone
> I'd forgotten were tyrannies;
> Even no need to fret
> About your diurnal tears.[38]

Mourning is the obligation of the living, not the dead; the modern dead are immune to the tears of the living. In poems like Fuller's "Ghost Voice," it is as if the venerated object of Wordsworth's poems to the mysterious Lucy, "Rolled round in earth's diurnal course, / With rocks and stones and trees," or the quixotic subject of Hardy's contrite elegies to his neglected wife, Emma, had come back to life to rebuke the poets for their excessive mourning and to beg the bereaved to leave them alone. The corpse poem's repudiation of the elegy, however, is not simultaneously a rejection of the dead. The corpse poem may disavow mourning, but this renegade poetic form more effectively raises the dead than elegy ever could, simply by lending them the agency of the poet's own voice. The dead live through the voice of the poet, creating the central and irresolvable contradiction of the corpse poem. Through prosopopoeia, poets reanimate the dead to instruct the living not to reanimate them. These "ghost voices" refuse reanimation *through* reanimation. If poets were to take the anti-elegiac theme of the corpse poem seriously, then there would no longer be not only elegies but corpse poems as well.

Ironically, it is the frustration and discomfort with the elegy that keeps the corpse poem alive. Recent corpse poems, many adopting the classical persona of Eurydice, draw their rhetorical force from a concerted attack upon the perceived excesses of the elegy. Peter Davison's "Eurydice in Darkness" (1966) prefers the company of her familiars (the three-headed lapdog, the river boatman, the gaggle of furies, and even the undertaker himself) to the "everlasting mooning and fiddling" of Orpheus's self-pitying dirges. This corpse poem depicts Orpheus, literature's paradigmatic elegist, as a self-absorbed narcissist "clinging to that lyre / As though the world depended on it." Fighting hard to preserve her death and to make it her own, Davison's Eurydice tricks the self-important Orpheus into facing her (and thus releasing her) from his sorrowful song, sending her laughing and spinning back to Hades. Pamela White Hadas's "Eurydice" (1979) is equally defiant, refusing outright to be the elegist's "dum dimwit ghost" following his "deathless voice" back to life. This second Eurydice, with her heartrending plea, "O Orpheus, let me be," also tricks her would-be redeemer into turning, securing her own freedom from the coercive melodies of that "damn hymn."[39]

The most memorable of the anti-Orpheus poems, H. D.'s "Eurydice" (1917), articulates this theme best, upbraiding the "arrogant" Orpheus not for failing to bring her back from the dead but for trying at all. "Hell is no worse than your earth," Eurydice informs the retreating Orpheus. At least in hell she stands out more distinctly against the colorless background than the bloodless Orpheus among the vibrant colors of the living: "I have the fervour of myself for a presence / and my own spirit for light."[40] Eurydice may be dead, but she is not absent; in the corpse poem, the dead are present, if only to themselves. The loss in the poem is merely the

Reviving . . . Corpses

loss of life's monopoly on presence. These latter-day Eurydices insist that the dead have their own way of being and their own forms of knowing. In each poem, the world of the modern dead is neither demonized nor idealized; it is simply poetically realized as a space well beyond the recuperative reach of elegy.

The Eurydice poems communicate to the elegist the same message that all the modern corpse poems ultimately seek to convey: please do not assume that what the dead really want is to return to the living. The modern dead do not regret their passing; they object only to the elegists' presumptuous if well-meaning attempts to deprive them of their deaths. If death has died in the twentieth century, has the overactive elegy, forever trying to restore the dead back to life, helped to ensure its demise? Orphic elegy may be less an homage to the dead than a self-indulgence of the living. By employing the unusual point of view of the mourned, and not the time-honored perspective of the mourner, the modern corpse poem assumes one of its most important strategic functions: a forum for critiquing the literary pretensions of the venerable but outmoded elegy.

And so we arrive at the chief purpose of the corpse poem, the reason for its tremendous vitality throughout the twentieth century. The main cultural and literary function of the modern corpse poem is to make dying "dying" once again. Speaking in the voices of the dead provides a way for poetry to make present a certain kind of absence. Corpse poems, unlike elegies, strive to reconstitute death, not to compensate for it. The corpse poem is not a substitute for loss but a vehicle for it, not a restitution for loss but a means to achieve it. The corpse poem can only dream about the luxury of the modern elegy to "practice losing farther, losing faster," to cite Elizabeth Bishop's haunting villanelle.[41] While the traditional elegy may be an "art of saving" and the modern elegy an "art of losing,"[42] the corpse poem constitutes neither a simple art of saving nor of losing but a complex art of saving loss itself. The corpse poem thus illustrates a more complicated and contradictory relation to loss than the elegy, which continues to rely heavily upon a binary of consolation and refusal that the corpse poem views as suspect in a world that hardly knows how to calculate its losses. Corpse poems are never freighted with the heavy loss that characterizes elegies because they are rarely elegizing anything, not even the demise of elegy itself, perceived as an anachronistic art form ill-suited to the age of genocide.

Grief and mourning, if they appear in the modern corpse poem at all, tend to be afterthoughts or asides, something that takes place outside the bounds of the poem. This is not to say that bereavement has nothing to do with the corpse poem, but only to suggest that mourning is less a central poetic motivation than an occasional thematic subject in a group of poems that more frequently inveigh against bereavement. If mourning were the chief motivation behind the corpse poem, one would expect to find a wealth of poems memorializing dead loved ones. Yet, in my recovery of speaking corpse poetry, I have uncovered not a single poem in which a poet ventriloquizes the voice of a deceased parent, child, sibling, lover, or friend. A poet's deceased family and friends provide singularly inappropriate subjects for the corpse poem's brazen fantasy of resuscitation. These dead are fundamentally irrecoverable; bringing them back to life would entail nothing less than a violent occupation and displacement that would kill them off all over again. Avoiding the emotional quicksand of personal attachment, corpse poems instead choose to reanimate more generic personalities: mythological figures like Icarus or Persephone, biblical figures like Abel or Lazarus, cultural figures like Elvira Shatayev or Matthew Shepard, or anonymous figures like soldiers or citizens.[43] The critical prerequisite of any corpse poem is distance, an emotional buffer separating the voice of the poet from the body of the corpse, as if to shield the poet from the contamination and contagion such proximity to the dead inevitably entails.

Composed at a secure remove from the emotional maelstrom of personal bereavement, most corpse poems lack the consider-

Reviving . . . Corpses

able affective power of elegy. The corpse poem, when it moves the reader, moves us through social outrage or philosophical argument, rarely through raw emotion. Although its central purpose is to restore to dying the gravitas that recent changes in the culture of death have so thoroughly trivialized, the corpse poem, no less than the elegy, may be responsible for contributing to death's demise. The sheer proliferation of corpse poems in the modern period is entirely symptomatic of the very problem these poems seek to resolve: the emptying out of mortality that deprives modern deaths of their singularity and distinction. After all, if the living can speak in the voice of the dead, then what exactly is unique or irreplaceable about death? A vacuous space any voice can fill, death in the twentieth century is completely up for grabs.

The corpse poem has an even more serious challenge to overcome in its unrealized mission to restore dying to its place of prominence and privilege. If the corpse poem has so far failed to cure the modern ailment of death without dying, then this failure can be attributed to the genre's own dependence upon, and routine restaging of, just such a problematic. The corpse poem is only possible in the first place because it permits the poet "To die - without the Dying." The chief question the corpse poem thus strives to settle—the death of dying—is in fact its condition of possibility. Insofar as the corpse poem endlessly repeats the very problem it addresses, the death of dying will never be undone, not so long, at any rate, as the corpse poem itself continues paradoxically to enact it.

poetic

I have addressed in my reading of the corpse poem the various ways in which poets temporarily give up their animate selves in order to channel, through poetic language, the voices of the dead. I conclude this literary exhumation by exploring more closely the intimate relation between the two terms "corpse" and "poem."

Chapter Two

Why, exactly, is a poem an appropriate vehicle for a corpse? The answer is in part stylistic. In its isolated, fragmented, and unnatural form, poetry resembles a Yeatsian "rag and bone shop."[44] The broken physicality of verse aligns poetry, more than any other literary genre, with corporeal disintegration. But there is more to the association of poems and cadavers than their shared structural dissolution. At a more fundamental level, poetry's concentrated attention to words and their histories highlights the status of all words as dead letters. "Our every word is a 'dead letter,' a dead language handed down to us by the dead," Giorgio Agamben eulogizes in *The End of the Poem*. As early as Augustine's *De Trinitate*, Agamben notes, to poeticize is to "experience the death of one's own language and one's own voice."[45] Insofar as poetic language is already dead language, my initial assertion that poets offer themselves up as mediums for the dead merely disguises the way death already speaks through the poet, through the medium of language itself.

Not every poet agrees that corpse and poem are completely homologous. Emily Dickinson, for one, remains unconvinced:

> A word is dead
> When it is said,
> Some say.
>
> I say it just
> Begins to live
> That day.   (P, 278)

Acknowledging through the rhyming of "dead" and "said" that language is indeed fatal, Dickinson nonetheless challenges the assumption that a poetic word is a dead word. Language inevitably brings death, she concedes, but to the poet, not the poem. Anticipating the philosophical interest in the demise of the writer enlivening such twentieth-century texts as Derrida's "Signature Event Context" and Roland Barthes's "The Death of the Author,"[46] Dickinson's use of passive voice in the first stanza implies that any

Reviving . . . Corpses

poem is readable without its author. In a poem, a word exists independently, signifies on its own; words communicate and circulate in the writer's absence. To the degree that all writing presumes the radical absence of the agent who produced it, philosophy's infamous "death of the author" can only be read as entirely redundant.

Poets after Dickinson, however, are on the whole deeply skeptical of poetry's reputed immortality. Writing in the shadow of mass extermination, Paul Celan, one of Dickinson's European translators, contradicts his predecessor's faith in the afterlife of language:

A word—you know:
a corpse.

Come let us wash it,
come let us comb it,
come let us turn
Its eye heavenward.[47]

Directly analogizing a word to a corpse, Celan invites his postwar readers to join him in preparing language for burial. Celan, who before the onset of World War II might have agreed with Dickinson that a word is not dead when it is said, after the war includes language in the death toll of genocide. Language cannot begin to explain the horrors of genocide since language is itself one of its victims. In Celan's understanding of the relation between language and death, words are corpses, and poems are coffins for language's remains.

Complicating the literary historical debate over a word's vitality, Sylvia Plath's poem "Stillborn" (1960) places poetry in an ambiguous space somewhere between life and death. For Plath, a poem is at once dead (stillborn) and alive (still born):

These poems do not live: it's a sad diagnosis.
They grew their toes and fingers well enough,
Their little foreheads bulged with concentration.

Chapter Two

> If they missed out on walking about like people
> It wasn't for any lack of mother-love.
>
> O I cannot understand what happened to them!
> They are proper in shape and number and every part.
> They sit so nicely in the pickling fluid!
> They smile and smile and smile and smile at me.
> And still the lungs won't fill and the heart won't start.[48]

"Stillborn" suggests that poems gestating in draft form are live poems, while completed poems are dead poems, fully formed but lifeless, like fetuses in pickling fluid. Because poems die before they are born, poets give birth to corpses. Poets, Plath implies, bring death to full term.

At first glance, "Stillborn" does not appear to be a corpse poem at all, at least as I have defined it here, for it does not directly employ the first-person voice of the speaking cadaver. And yet Plath speaks in the first person through the poem itself, through the agency of the dead fetus that she mourns. By the end of the poem, poet and poem, mother and fetus, living and dead have effectively changed places:

> They are not pigs, they are not even fish,
> Though they have a piggy and a fishy air—
> It would be better if they were alive, and that's what they were.
> But they are dead, and their mother near dead with distraction,
> And they stupidly stare, and do not speak of her.

Plath's "I" becomes "their mother" and her "me" becomes a "her," grammatically reversing the poem's subject and object positions. In a subtle chiasmatic reversal, the fetus lends voice to the now-muted poet. Plath's poems do not speak "*of* her," but they are the only things speaking *for* her. Ironically, Plath can speak in the poem only through the agency of the dead words she memorializes. Here we find the deepest and most disturbing connection between corpses and poems. Strictly speaking, it may not in fact be

Reviving . . . Corpses

the case that the poet, through language, animates the dead. More accurately, it appears that it is the stillborn words of poetry that animate the poet. Poets are not serving as mediums for the dead; they are themselves dead without the poem to give them voice. Death thus animates the living, not the other way around, which is why a poet inhabiting the role of the speaking cadaver may not, in the end, be such a paradox after all.

The corpse poem as a specific poetic type tells us something important about literature as a whole: poetry can ventriloquize the dead because literature, as a medium, already incorporates death. The individual corpse poems I have examined in this chapter collectively pose a larger question about the status of all literature. Is not every literary utterance a speaking corpse, a disembodied voice detached from a living, breathing body? Literature that immortalizes voice also entombs it, which is why every poem can be broadly understood as a corpse poem. The speaking corpse names not just a particular kind of literary persona but a general attribute of all lyric poems, verse suspended between the animated voice of the speaker and the frozen form of the poem that preserves it.

Lyric poetry has always been one of the preeminent cultural mediums for the resuscitation of the dead. Yet in the nineteenth and twentieth centuries, sound and sight technologies like the photograph, gramophone, telephone, radio, and film can each legitimately claim to revive the dead more effectively than the poem. Where the cultural work of reanimation is concerned, poetry has become in the past two hundred years a dead medium, superseded and displaced by far more powerful technologies of resurrection. The trope of the speaking corpse is thus for poetry, and perhaps for all literature, an entirely self-reflexive one. In the final analysis, the speaking corpse operates as a figure for poetry itself, a dead voice that refuses to remain silent, a spectral genre that continues to speak and walk abroad.

3
Surviving . . . Lovers

If the last-word poem moves through elegy, and the speaking corpse poem travels beyond elegy, the surviving lover poem circles back to elegy. It is the reemergence in the modern period of the dawn song, one of the most archaic of poetic forms, that helps to revive the dying elegy, reminding us that, in truth, elegies have never been just about dying and reviving. They have also been powerful mediums of surviving.

My final chapter, on the surviving voice in modern poetry, proceeds from the premise that poems of loss often simultaneously function as narratives of awakening—as the centuries old confusion of "mourning" and "morning" might suggest.[1] The homonym is not unimportant, for the conflation of mourning and morning, of loss and awakening, articulates a central tension at the heart of not just the modern elegy but yet another equally expressive, though curiously overlooked, genre: the modern aubade. The aubade shares important affinities with the elegy; indeed, the aubade, I will suggest, may even be a form of elegy. Perhaps more than any other poetic genre, the aubade marries eros and thanatos, joining together love and loss in a centuries-old drama of lovers parting at sunrise.

Originally a minor medieval lyric form, the aubade (Old French), alba (Old Provençal), or *Tagelied* (German) follows the simplest of plots. A knight and a lady risk everything for a night of passion; awoken at dawn by sunlight, birdsong, or watchman, the knight must escape detection and return to battle, leaving the beloved behind to mourn her lover's absence and to hope for his

Surviving . . . Lovers

eventual return. Spoken in the voice of lady, knight, or watchman (and sometimes all three), the aubade wages battle against the break of day and the separation of lovers. Unlike the more common chanson, in which a knight pines for a lady he can never have, the alba or aubade celebrates the consummation of forbidden love and laments its sudden interruption. Consider this late twelfth- or early thirteenth-century medieval aubade, spoken from the point of view of the lady:

> Cant voi l'aube dou jor venir,
> Nulle rien ne doi tant haïr,
> K'elle fait de moi departir
> Mon amin cui j'ain per amors.
> Or ne hais riens tant com le jour,
> Amins, ke me depairt de vos.
>
> Je ne vos puis de jor veoir,
> Car trop redout l'apercevoir,
> Et se vos di trestout por voir
> K'en agait sont li envious.
> Or ne hais riens tant com le jour,
> Amins, ke me depairt de vos.
>
> Quant je me gix dedens mon lit
> Et je resgairde encoste mi,
> Je n'i truis poent de mon amin,
> Se m'en plaing a fins amerous.
> Or ne hais riens tant com le jour,
> Amins, ke me depairt de vos.
>
> Biaus dous amis, vos en ireis:
> A Deu soit vos cors comandeis.
> Por Deu vos pri, ne m'oblieis:
> Je n'ain nulle rien tant com vos.
> Or ne hais riens tant com le jour,
> Amins, ke me depairt de vos.

Chapter Three

>Or pri a tous les vrais amans
>Ceste chanson voixent chantant
>Ens en despit des medixans
>Et des mavais maris jalous.
>Or ne hais riens tant com lou jour,
>Amins, ke me depairt de vos.

Nothing is more hateful to me than to see the dawn appear, for dawn snatches my true love from my side. How I hate the break of day which parts me, dear, from you! // All day long I dare not see you, for fear our love should be discovered. And indeed I tell you truly that envious ones are on the watch for us. How I hate the break of day which parts me, dear, from you. // When I lie in my bed and look beside me and cannot find my dear one, then I make my plaint to all true lovers. How I hate the break of day which parts me, dear, from you! // Fair sweet friend, you must go; God have you in his keeping; and I beg of you in God's name, do not forget me, for I love you above all things. How I hate the break of day which parts me, dear, from you! // Now I pray all true lovers that they will sing this song, despite all slanderers and wicked husbands. How I hate the break of day which parts me, dear, from you![2]

This impassioned utterance takes the very specific form of a protest or lament, a "plaint to all true lovers."[3] Intended to be sung at the break of dawn, the erotic alba bemoans the cessation of sexual love while acknowledging the inevitability of time, change, and mortality. Yet, tellingly, no standardized metrical pattern distinguishes the medieval aubade. Unlike the elegy that originates precisely as a type of meter (couplets comprised of alternating hexameter and pentameter lines), the aubade has no identifiable verse form of its own.[4] Aubades are recognizable as such only by their brief titles, which immediately and economically invoke for their audience an entire dramatic situation. Like the nocturnal lovers hostile to the approach of day and the responsibilities it must bring, the aubade refuses metrically to mark its own time, refuses, in its own way, to collude in the lovers' inevitable separation. In a world of rigid binaries—unity and separation, night and day, ecstasy and grief—the aubade throws in its lot with the lovers, enacting its own drama of denial and deferral. Offering a place of timeless refuge, the aubade operates exactly like an elegy, allowing the separated lovers to occupy, for just a little while longer, the shared space of a lyric haven.

In the first full-length critical study of the medieval dawn song, Jonathan Saville reads both the chanson and the aubade as poems of grief: "in one case, grief for what one does not have; and in the other, grief for what one has and now must lose."[5] In structure, theme, and tone, the aubade is fundamentally a tragedy; the dawn always comes, the world always intrudes, and pleasure does not last forever. For the knight no less than the lady, the "thought of dawn is grievous," while "the sorrow that daytime brings grieves ... still more." Another aubade knight echoes the same sentiment, tenderly explaining to his lover, "sweet one, whatever they tell you, do not believe that there is any grief like the parting of lovers, for I myself have proved it."[6] While the melancholic aubade anxiously acknowledges the inevitability of passion's demise, it nonetheless labors to prolong love's reach through the agency of the lyric's own utterance.

In this final chapter I explore the complex relation between elegy and aubade by focusing on the persistence of dawn songs in the modern period. Seemingly the most unmodern of subjects, the aubade's core theme of true love recurs with surprising frequency in postromantic poetry. A love lyric known more for its late medieval and Renaissance revivals (Chaucer's *Troilus and Criseyda*, Shakespeare's *Romeo and Juliet*, Donne's "The Sunne Rising"), the aubade emerges as a major if understudied verse form in the poetry of Robert Browning, Algernon Charles Swinburne, Stevie Smith, W. B. Yeats, Ezra Pound, Richard Wilbur, Philip Larkin, and Elizabeth Bishop (among others).[7] But what exactly attracts a modern writer, ostensibly committed to an aesthetic of originality and experimentation, to the highly conventional and repetitive narrative of a troubadour love lyric? I argue that the aubade's valuation of love over loss, but also self over other, is central to the appeal of this archaic form for modernist poets intrigued by the elegiac possibilities of memorializing lost passion. In the end, however, the aubade's greatest attraction may be its radical potential to ethically outdo the elegy, finally and fully resisting elegy's most selfish impulse: to reverse the hands of time and to restore the dead to life.

loving

I begin not with a poet but with a theorist, perhaps the only great philosopher of the aubade. Roland Barthes's exquisite *Fragments d'un discours amoureux* (1977; translated into English in 1978 as *A Lover's Discourse: Fragments*) offers a veritable primer for lovers who must part. Composed in broken fragments, and spoken from the viewpoint of the lover left behind, *A Lover's Discourse* constitutes its own lyric protest, an aubade in prose. No less rigid in its formulation than the medieval alba, the lover's discourse neatly divides the world into two: the "you" who leaves and the "I" who remains, the other who departs and the subject who waits, the beloved who forgets and the lover who remembers. By vocation, the beloved is "migrant, fugitive," while the lover is "sedentary, motionless." If "the other is in a condition of perpetual departure," the subject is "nailed to the spot, in suspense—like a package in some forgotten corner of a railway station." Part crucified martyr, part discarded commodity, the amorous subject never stops waiting and hoping for the return of the fugitive other. For Barthes, it could not be otherwise: "Amorous absence functions in a single direction, expressed by the one who stays, never by the one who leaves: an always present *I* is constituted only by confrontation with an always absent *you*."[8]

It is an old and even objectionable story, for to suffer from the

Surviving... Lovers

beloved's absence is to be "miraculously feminized" (ALD, 14), turned into a waiting Penelope for every wandering Odysseus. To fall in love is immediately to occupy the space of femininity, immobility, and receptivity. Yet Barthes claims femininity not as an invitation to despair but as an incitement to artistry; it is woman who weaves and sings, "woman who gives shape to absence." An amorous subject perpetually in love, continually desiring, forever anticipating, Barthes waits. And while he waits, he writes.

Barthes's definition of love is archaic in more than a classical or literary sense; it is also, at base, a theory of child mourning: "As a child I didn't forget: interminable days, abandoned days, when the mother was working far away" (ALD, 14). Barthes waits for her at the bus stop, but "the buses would pass one after the other, she wasn't in any of them" (15). Like the forlorn package in the train station, Barthes's forgotten boy at the bus stop goes nowhere, rooted to the spot, waiting, desiring, remembering. *A Lover's Discourse* locates the origin of love in the birth of melancholia. Unlike little Ernst, who expertly manages his mother's departures through the game of *fort-da*, Barthes refuses to find a maternal substitute, rejects the consolations of compensation, and insists on reuniting with the original love object. For the faithful aubade lover Barthes himself epitomizes, love is nothing more, and nothing less, than the wish to be taken along.

Waiting anxiously for the other's return, the lover enacts what Barthes calls a "minor mourning" (ALD, 37). Fear that the absent other may already be dead impels not just the lover's discourse but also the poet's aubade: "it is the fear of a mourning which has already occurred, at the very origin of love" (30). For Barthes, love is elegy.[9] Like many modern elegies, the Barthesian aubade expresses open hostility toward the absent love object, demanding of the errant beloved: "turn back, look at me, see what you have made of me" (33). But Barthes's reproach falls on deaf ears; in the end, Barthesian love is unrequited love. There can never be, in Barthes's world, two lovers who wait, or two lovers who leave. The

Chapter Three

Barthesian lover is convinced that he alone waits, that he alone is in love. The proof is in the action: those who abandoned him never could have done so had their love been true (*vrai*).

In the middle of *A Lover's Discourse*, in a fragment titled "*écrire*" ("to write"), Barthes writes about waiting, trying his hand at love poetry for the first and only time in the book. The result is three haikus — each penned in the spirit of the Japanese poet Bashō and each, strikingly, an aubade:

> Ce matin d'été, beau temps sur le golfe,
> Je suis sorti
> Cueillir une glycine.
>
> Ce matin d'été, beau temps sur le golfe,
> Je suis resté longtemps à ma table,
> Sans rien faire.
>
> Ce matin, beau temps sure le golfe,
> Je suis resté immobile
> A penser à l'absent.
>
> This summer morning, the bay sparkling,
> I went outside
> To pick a wisteria.
>
> This summer morning, the bay sparkling,
> I'm still a long time at my table
> Nothing to do.
>
> This morning, the bay sparkling,
> I stayed here, motionless,
> Thinking of who is gone.[10] (ALD, 97)

All three poems convey a sense of mute loss. In the first, Barthes emulates Walt Whitman's famous mourner and picks a flower, acknowledging the break; in the second, he remains idling at his table, nothing to do; and in the third, he remains entirely motion-

Surviving . . . Lovers

less, lost in memory.[11] In the sparkling morning light that characterizes so many dawn songs, Barthes chronicles his fall into melancholy—into a static though not unproductive interiority. The writing of not one but three aubades constitutes the abandoned lover's latest attempt to kill time, to escape change, and to keep the beloved close. Only a lover left behind would attempt such folly, would spend a beautiful sunny morning dallying in aubades. For Barthes, the aubade is every bit a *lover's* discourse. (The beloved, Barthes recognizes, has better things to do than to write, or read, a "mild little haiku" [ALD, 98].) These trial aubades, however, will never succeed in calling the other back, and they will not alleviate the lover's suffering through the work of substitution and replacement. In a rare and radical refusal of the psychoanalytic theory of love, loss, and language, Barthes declares that "writing compensates for nothing, sublimates nothing" (100). Deeply anticompensatory, the humble aubade is really an anti-elegy at heart, a pointless exercise in waiting.

Why, then, write an aubade? Indeed, why write at all? If, as Barthes perceptively suggests, compensation or sublimation is not the aim of the aubade, then what does this lyric verse form seek to achieve? In the following pages I hope to answer this question by surveying a range of nineteenth- and twentieth-century aubades, paying particular attention to their precise modes of speaking and address. Who speaks in the modern aubade, and to whom do they speak? What recurrent tropes, tenses, or techniques distinguish the aubade? And what exactly accounts for the marriage of elegy and aubade?

In its simplest definition, the aubade is a poetry of uncoupling. Yet the Barthesian couple, comprised of the one who leaves and the one who waits, fails to exhaust both the specific types of uncoupling and the full diversity of lovers' discourses explored by modern poetry. Barthes's discourse of love respects the pain only of the one who waits, thus privileging just one particular form of the traditional aubade while simultaneously foreclosing its more

Chapter Three

multiform, mobile, and modern incarnations. In this chapter I probe four of the most common types of modern dawn songs, each addressing a different scenario: a lover who stays, a lover who leaves, two lovers who stay, and a lover who wakes alone. These four different movements—waiting, leaving, refusing, and existing—offer modern readers strategies and philosophies for surviving lost love. When all is said and suffered, the aubade is about nothing if not survival, the ability to endure when the other is nowhere to be found.

waiting

Given Barthes's insistence that love poetry is the vocation only of the one who waits, it is striking that very few modern aubades adopt the position of the lover left behind; indeed, of the hundreds of modern aubades I have surveyed, only a handful attempt to give voice to the waiting lover. Even more surprising, most of these poems are in fact dialogues, ventriloquizing the voices both of lover and beloved, lady and knight. These modern albas follow the medieval formula exactly, retaining each of the genre's key features: an enclosed love chamber, an aura of sexual intimacy, a cock's crow or a bird's song, a protest against the break of dawn, and a contest of will between lovers. Central to the poem's dramatic action is a debate over whether dawn has in fact arrived and the beloved must indeed depart. Composed in the wake of World War I, when lovers were parted in tragic numbers, these poems find in the medieval aubade an invitation to explore modernism's own preoccupation with the tension between pleasure and reality. Freud's *Beyond the Pleasure Principle* (1923) sums up, in its very title, the philosophy of the aubade's fugitive beloved, who, in awaking to the call of reality, turns his back on the continuing demands of eros. Yet by refusing to silence the waiting lover who remains fully and unconditionally committed to pleasure, the dialogue aubades take Freud one step farther, imagining possibilities for

Surviving . . . Lovers

what might be called "beyond the reality principle."[12] Through the aubade, love, in its most intense and intimate forms, survives the cynicism, fatalism, and nihilism that allegedly distinguish modern love poetry from its more genteel Victorian predecessors. In the classic aubade, eros gives voice to its own reality, challenging any easy conquest of truth over delusion, knowledge over desire.

Two aubades from the interwar years, Stevie Smith's "Aubade" (1937) and W. B. Yeats's "Parting" (1933), model themselves directly on the medieval dawn song. Stevie Smith, in one of her earliest poems, begins her dialogue with the voice of the soon-to-be abandoned lover:

> My dove, my doe,
> I love you so,
> I cannot will not
> Let you go,
> 'Tis not the day lights yonder sky
> It is too soon
> I hear the cock's discordant cry,
> He doodles to the moon.
> It is not day
> I say
> It is the moon.[13]

The lover's protest that it is night and not day does not deny the reality of dawn so much as refigure it. Recognizing that dawn has in fact arrived, this lover's creative reinterpretation of the sights and sounds of the morning seeks to detain her beloved through a poetry of prevarication. For the aubade lover, however, such lying is never denying; it is instead an embrace of the reality of erotic love, which makes every day a night and every sun a moon.

Interestingly, it is the poem's spokesman for the reality principle who indulges in the aubade's greatest flights of fancy. Ostensibly speaking truth to delusion, the departing lover turns to classical mythology to justify his departure:

Chapter Three

> Alas, my love it is the day,
> Born twin to sun, but opening first
> The womb of night.
> There lies the day,
> Her cheeks are gray,
> Alas so soon it is the day.
> And now in agony her dam will try
> To bring forth sun, and in fulfillment die.
> No easy birth is here,
> Before our eyes
> Night bleeds
> And, born caesareanwise,
> Her son in flaming gear
> Comes forth and her succeeds.
> Once more for man the heavenly twins are born,
> Farewell, my love, adieu, it is the dawn.[14]

Invoking the Greek myth of Nyx, goddess of night and mother of day, Smith's departing lover paints a bloody portrait of dawn's arrival. After quietly birthing a gray-cheeked day, night expires in agony as a red-flamed sun hemorrhages forth. Reality emerges in this aubade as one long and labored conceit, a flight of figuration that turns the dawn song into a contest not between pleasure and reality but between twin versions of pleasure. In the modern aubade, the difference between loving and leaving is rather like the difference between Smith's day and sun: borne out of the same dark place, they emerge as two distinct yet related ways of being in the world.

But although the arguments for both staying and going are given their due in the classic aubade, one side invariably wins the argument. In Smith's "Aubade," it is the departing lover who silences his partner's complaints with the finality of a double goodbye: "Farewell, my love, adieu, it is the dawn." But in Yeats's memorable poem "Parting," it is the woman who gets the last word and pleasure that wins the day.

Surviving . . . Lovers

> *He.* Dear, I must be gone
> While night shuts the eyes
> Of the household spies;
> That song announces dawn.
>
> *She.* No, night's bird and love's
> Bids all true lovers rest,
> While his loud song reproves
> The murderous stealth of day.
>
> *He.* Daylight already flies
> From mountain crest to crest
>
> *She.* That light is from the moon.
>
> *He.* That bird . . .
>
> *She.* Let him sing on,
> I offer to love's play
> My dark declivities.[15]

In its dramatic staging and familiar dialogue, Yeats's "Parting" would appear to be a classic aubade, complete with a household of spies, a morning bird song, and an argument between lovers. Yet what distinguishes this aubade from nearly all others in the modern canon is that the man's nod to reality is quickly outmatched by the woman's call to pleasure. His perfect rhyme of "gone" and "dawn" comes entirely undone by her "sing on." Reality can't compete with pleasure, or rather, pleasure offers the greater reality: the irresistible pull of the lover's "dark declivities." Through the fast fall of alliteration, the entire poem enacts the downward slope connoted by the poem's sexually charged, polysyllabic last word, sliding from "dear" to "dawn" to "day" to "daylight" before smoothly entering her "dark declivities." In the end, the "parting" of the poem's title comes to signify not leaving but loving, the profound intimacy of renewed sexual passion.

89

Chapter Three

leaving

The voice of the departing lover, already present in these classic aubades, is an impossible utterance. For Barthes, a lover's discourse can never be spoken by the one who leaves, for waiting constitutes the very definition of love: "'Am I in love? – Yes, since I'm waiting'" (ALD, 39). Insisting that real love can only be borne out of abandonment and suffering, Barthes maintains "the ego discourses only when it is hurt" and "the fulfilled lover has no need to write" (55, 56). Yet a wealth of modern aubades, written entirely from the point of view of the lover who leaves, reveal that departing lovers may also be "hurt" and that even "fulfilled" lovers write aubades. To be sure, some modern poets adopt the convention of the departing lover to declare their sexual independence. But most turn to the aubade in a final attempt to hold on to the one they must eventually relinquish. Interestingly, both types of lyrics manage to keep the other present, to carry their partners a little ways with them, even and especially as they labor to forget them.

Of all the aubades written in the voice of a departing lover, Robert Browning's aubade in miniature, "Parting at Morning" (1845), comes closest to severing its ties altogether to the woman left behind.

> Round the cape of a sudden came the sea,
> And the sun looked over the mountain's rim:
> And straight was a path of gold for him,
> And the need of a world of men for me.[16]

A companion poem to "Meeting at Night," a serena or evening song about a sailor who steals away for a night onshore with his lover, Browning's "Parting at Morning" dramatizes the outcome of this secret tryst: the sailor, awoken by the sun, longs to return to the world of men. Never named or given voice, his female lover is present mainly by her absence; she is already, it would seem, a distant memory. The strong gerund in the poem's title suggests that

Surviving . . . Lovers

the leave-taking is only now taking place and that indeed the poem itself seeks to effect the necessary break. Browning's kinetic opening, with its hard stress on "round," turns the poem itself around, like a surging frigate rounding Cape Horn or a rising sun cresting a mountain. Yet, significantly, though the parting has begun, it is never actually completed in the aubade. Instead, the highly concentrated poem enacts a push-pull of movement and stasis: the quatrain's strong use of parataxis ("And" at the beginnings of lines) and the absence of internal punctuation propel the speaker forward in a rush of excitement and anticipation, while the sudden end-stops that conclude each line repeatedly and reluctantly bring the speaker up short, postponing the final parting to a space and time outside the poem itself. Tense, syntax, even audience (to whom is this poem addressed?) conspire to hold the restless lover back, complicating any easy narrative of adventure and escape.

In his own dramatization of the moment "Before Parting" (1866), Swinburne turns to the aubade to explain why Browning's sailor (or any aubade lover) must leave the one he professes to love. Simply put, one grows weary of too much sweetness:

> A month or twain to live on honeycomb
> Is pleasant; but one tires of scented time,
> Cold sweet recurrence of accepted rhyme,
> And that strong purple juice and foam
> Where the wine's heart has burst;
> Nor feel the latter kisses like the first.[17]

A devotee of passion, yet a realist all the same, Swinburne's departing lover is intensely conscious of "the bitter taste ensuing on the sweet." In a poem awash in oral imagery, this disenchanted lover decides that, in the end, it is better that love's sweet harvest be cleanly "scythèd" than carelessly trampled. Surprisingly, it is Swinburne's departing lover who sounds most like Barthes's waiting lover, at the moment when he recognizes in the beloved what Barthes calls the "speck of corruption" (*un point de corruption*).

91

Chapter Three

> I know not how this last month leaves your hair
> Less full of purple colour and hid spice,
> And that luxurious trouble of closed eyes
> Is mixed with meaner shadows and waste care;
> And love, kissed out by pleasure, seems not yet
> Worth patience to regret.[18]

To be even momentarily disillusioned by the other, now "mixed with meaner shadows and waste care," is to drop out of love and to fall back into reality. Swinburne's aubade, like so many departing lover monologues, originates out of this precise moment of "de-fascination" (*défasciné*), the moment when dawn shines a bright light on the beloved's sleeping body, whose closed eyes, limp hair, and etched face already forecast the corpse she will become.[19] More cynical than any later modernist, Swinburne's Victorian lover addresses his argument to a woman who can neither hear nor respond, reducing the aubade's traditional contest of wills to a simple, solitary, and perhaps selfish act of poetic and public self-justification.

Ezra Pound's depiction of the female body in his poem "Alba" (1913–15) powerfully if subtly conveys this same undeniable whiff of decay:

> As cool as the pale wet leaves
>   of lily-of-the-valley
> She lay beside me in the dawn.[20]

Another Eastern-inspired haiku, this perfect imagist poem relies on its title to provide dramatic context. Comprised (like Browning's aubade) solely of one or two syllable words, Pound's entire alba operates as a single simile, condensing the woman's cool, wet body with the damp of the dew-laden dawn. Pound's avoidance of internal punctuation and end-stops, together with his heavy use of the alliterative "l," creates a poem as limp and languid as the body it describes. Like the dew, the poem is itself fragile, impermanent,

Surviving . . . Lovers

effervescent. Indeed, as the past tense of the poem's only verb suggests, dawn has already passed and the lover has already departed. Importantly, the woman's postcoital body is recalled rather than observed, indicating that this departing lover still carries with him a strong sensory impression of passion's final distillation.

Pound's specific choice of a "lily-of-the-valley" as his central metaphor signifies more than the pale May flower so often depicted in aubades; connoting the white of death as well as the white of dawn, it recognizes and respects, in a single highly charged image, the profound sorrow of the woman left behind. In the Christian allegory of flowers, the lily of the valley springs up from a woman's tears—in one version Eve's tears when she is expelled from the Garden of Eden, and in another version the Virgin Mary's tears when Christ is hung on the cross.[21] Associated with both corruption and purity, Pound's lily of the valley, with its "pale wet leaves," further invokes the Greek mythological origins of dew, yet another story of female mourning. Memnon's death at the hands of Achilles causes his mother Eos such grief that her tears blanket the earth with dew. Dew thus comes into being as the sign of maternal sorrow, tears of mourning for a son taken too soon. The dawn song's very roots confuse morning and mourning, as day weeps itself into being.[22]

In more contemporary aubades, the classical and biblical associations of the dawn, respectfully invoked by Smith and gently hinted at by Pound, begin to lose their luster. Late twentieth-century aubades describe, most often, the claustrophobic predictability and inescapable tedium of early morning workday rituals. Indeed, of all the different types of departing lover aubades, the suburban commuter aubade is the most common and ultimately the most caustic. As modernity's vehicle of choice, the automobile, with its slamming doors and revving engines, replaces the watchman's call or the bird's song to usher in the day. "No cocks crow in suburbia," Karl Shapiro writes in his "Aubade," though "the steering wheel is sticky with dew," and "it is always dawn when I say goodnight to you."[23] Gregory Orr goes farther, confusing cars with coffins: "Up and down the street the sound / of coffins closing. / No, it's only / car doors slamming, people off to work." Instead of heading off to epic battle, Orr's hapless suburban husbands are caught in the daily grind of alienated labor:

> Here, lawns are shorn
> and Samson's trapped
> In the daily round:
> chained to the mill,
> he grinds his enemies' corn.[24]

Industrial production and global capitalism have supplanted heroic battle and chivalric romance as love's new reality. "Lilies" belong to "some other world," Orr laments, one far removed from a suburban life marked, as the poem's reference to Samson and its rhyme of "shorn" and "corn" insist, less by sexual fulfillment than sexual castration. In the modern commuter aubade, shackled male suburbanites bemoan their inability to be true departing lovers, to go beyond what Shapiro calls the "loaded ashtrays," "rust neckties," and "divorced mattresses" of a "newspaper dawn." But they also understand that leaving has its costs, the loss of "naked breasts," "earthquake thighs," and "electric mouth[s]" that make their modern servitude survivable.

In the end, departing lover aubades are nothing if not ambivalent. Typically, these lovers on the move are torn between the desire to stay and the need to go. Painting a far more complicated picture than Barthes's portrait of modern love allows, the aubade poet sees the full difficulty of departing, carefully anatomizing in the drama of uncoupling the losses and not just the gains. Some departing lovers even express empathy for the lover they leave behind; others come to the realization that leaving is itself a form of waiting, an act of self-injury that leaves them, too, in a state of anxiety and anticipation. As Nicholas Samaras puts it in his airplane aubade: "One may leave / but two are left."[25] What then

Surviving . . . Lovers

would make a lover return or refuse to leave in the first place? How do we account for those aubades where neither lover departs, and no one is left waiting? How, in other words, does an aubade itself come apart?

refusing

Although lyrics in which no one leaves are far less numerous than the departing lover poems, they nonetheless comprise a coherent subset of the modern aubade. These poems operate as anti-aubades, dawn songs in which the amorous couple, knowing fully what is expected of them, simply refuse to follow the script, electing to challenge fate, remain in bed, and let dawn pass by. Anti-aubades neither refuse reality nor surrender to it; instead, they cautiously carve out their own reality, testing the waters for a new kind of dawn song in which pleasure may be the only reality that matters in the end. These poems dare to ask what the medieval aubade never did: What would happen if the claim of love was finally to win out over the call of duty?

The anti-aubade's initial answer would appear to be "nothing much." Harvey Shapiro writes of men watching from bed as naked "women rise in their glory / to go to the john," returning with nothing lost, nothing gained.[26] And Jeff Worley composes a "Sunday Aubade" in which he lounges in bed distracted by his Sunday crossword puzzle, with his "wife, nakedly indiscreet, wondering where's breakfast."[27] Yet what's missing from these domestic poems is any real sign of sexual ardor. The choice to ignore the warning calls of dawn prove to have consequences after all, the loss of the very thing aubade lovers struggle hardest to preserve—passion.

Perhaps this is why Adelaide Crapsey, in her "Aubade," cautions against turning a blind eye or a deaf ear to dawn's sensory awakening:

> The morning is new and the skies are fresh washed with light,
> The day cometh in with the sun and I awake laughing.

Chapter Three

> Hasten belovèd!
> For see, while you were yet sleeping
> The cool and virgin feet of dawn went soundless over grey
>   meadows,
> And the earth is requickened under her touch.
> The vision that came with gradual steps departeth in an instant;
> Hasten, lest it be unbeheld of your eyes.[28]

In this joyous poem, one lover wakes another, not to announce his or her own departure but to witness the fleet passing of dawn. Here the arrival of dawn functions less as an urgent warning than as a critical opportunity, an occasion to behold the exact moment of revitalization that makes the world, and love itself, "new." To miss dawn is to miss the chance to renew passion. Crapsey's jubilant lovers understand that desire itself is fugitive and that the best way to preserve pleasure is not to ignore reality but to acknowledge it as the very thing that "requickens" love.

And it is never too late to requicken love, as Richard Wilbur's "A Late Aubade," one of the most serene aubades in the canon of modern dawn songs, lyrically attests. The poem's title resonates in at least four different ways: a late morning aubade, a late in life aubade, a recent aubade, or even a dead aubade. Wilbur's anti-aubade, in which he and his wife elect to spend the day in bed, appears to circumvent the convention of both the lovers' traditional quarrel and their inevitable separation:

> You could be sitting now in a carrel
> Turning some liver-spotted page,
> Or rising in an elevator-cage
> Toward Ladies' Apparel.
>
> You could be planting a raucous bed
> Of salvia, in rubber gloves,
> Or lunching through a screed of someone's loves
> With pitying head.

Surviving . . . Lovers

> Or making some unhappy setter
> Heel, or listening to a bleak
> Lecture on Schoenberg's serial technique.
> Isn't this better?[29]

Sitting, turning, rising, planting, lunching, making, listening — the many participles in the poem's first three stanzas powerfully manifest the grammar that governs all aubades. Cast in the present tense but all preceded by the conditional "could," these participles perfectly capture the tension between action and stasis that defines every dawn song. The two participles that recur most frequently in dawn songs — waiting and parting — together invoke the state of suspended animation that Barthes identifies as the very definition of loving.

In Wilbur's aubade, the piling of participles in the poem's opening conditional stanzas imagine all the activities his wife might be doing in an ordinary day: reading, shopping, gardening, lunching, dog walking, or, most revealingly, listening to a lecture on "Schoenberg's serial technique." The reference to Schoenberg's method of ordering twelve notes in a row to unify a melody offers Wilbur a way to harmonize all the major themes of the aubade — time, sound, duration, rhythm, progression, repetition, and, finally, completion. But it is a "bleak lecture" even so, and one both lovers have chosen to miss. This connubial couple turns away from life's daily routine, preferring not to waste time but to save it, expending energy only on their passion:

> Think of all the time you are not
> Wasting, and would not care to waste,
> Such things, thank God, not being to your taste.
> Think what a lot
>
> Of time, by woman's reckoning,
> You've saved, and so may spend on this,
> You who had rather lie in bed and kiss
> Than anything.

> It's almost noon, you say? If so,
> Time flies, and I need not rehearse
> The rosebuds-theme of centuries of verse.
> If you *must* go,
>
> Wait for a while, then slip downstairs
> And bring us up some chilled white wine,
> And some blue cheese, and crackers, and some fine
> Ruddy-skinned pears.[30]

Wilbur's logic is seductive: if "time flies," then why must lovers? So much better to stay in bed and feast past noon on wine, cheese, crackers, and pears.

And yet even Wilbur's sweetly satisfied dawn song cannot entirely escape the ominous notes that make his late aubade so poignantly elegiac: the wine is "chilled" and "white," the cheese is "blue," and the pears are "ruddy-skinned" or ripe. More still life than dawn song, the poem's final stanza cannot help but to bring out the "hearse" in "rehearse," the recognition that any serial technique, as every poet knows, must finally reach termination. Wilbur, in part through the writing of the aubade itself, has merely succeeded in pushing the inevitable moment of the lovers' separation forward in time. By the poem's final stanzas, the future conditional has already subsided, replaced by an encroaching present tense. An aubade may be "late," but it is never *too* late. Eventually, when reality dawns, one lover will wake alone.

existing

Single-lover aubades are the most existential of all modern dawn songs. They are also the most explicitly elegiac. Left alone with no possibility of the beloved's return, the speakers of these lonely aubades awake into full awareness of their present solitude or of their own future vanishing. Waking assumes in these poems the full burden of its double meaning: to come to consciousness is to begin

Surviving . . . Lovers

once more the act of mourning. These dolorous dawn songs rue the passing not so much of lost loves as lost selves—selves that used to be and selves that will never be. They commemorate, in other words, the many acts of self-delusion and self-departure that expose even self-love to the agony of a lover's discourse.

For the one who wakes alone, dawn marks the assumption of irredeemable and nearly indescribable losses—losses not darkly anticipated but painfully resumed with each successive sunrise. Every new day to an aging John Payne shines a spotlight on a lifetime of dreams unrealized: "Amber of dawn, thou bringest me scant pleasure; / . . . Thy gold is as the wraith of bygone hope / Poured without measure / Upon the upland meadows of my youth." Lamenting lost opportunities, bygone hopes, and chronic disappointments, Payne dismisses the streaming rays of dawn as mere "wraiths . . . of old deceptive glory" and the aubade itself as no more than a murderous "false story." What's left, for this solitary speaker, is neither passion nor grief but fear—"fear, that doth steep with such a venomed juice / The cup of being."[31]

Philip Larkin's justly famous "Aubade" identifies this waking fear more precisely: dread of one's own complete annihilation. As if in response to Payne's plaintive regrets over a wasted life, Larkin summons what his insomniac self knows to be a far greater horror:

> Waking at four to soundless dark, I stare.
> In time the curtain edges will grow light.
> Till then I see what's really always there:
> Unresting death, a whole day nearer now.[32]

Seized by the terror of dying, and being dead, Larkin's mind blanks "at the total emptiness forever / the sure extinction /. . . Not to be here, Not to be anywhere." Freud insists that while it is entirely possible to imagine a beloved's sudden disappearance from the world, our unconscious protects us from ever truly envisioning our own demise: "at bottom no one believes in his own death . . . [for] in the unconscious every one of us is convinced of his own immortality."[33] Aubade poets know better. In the soundless early morning dark, alone with one's own thoughts, the thing that "stays just on the edge of vision," or what Larkin calls "a small unfocused blur, a standing chill," flashes into consciousness.

Dawn represents the day's single most dangerous moment, the relay between unconscious and conscious states of being, when knowledge of nonbeing, of one's own impending insensate state, can no longer be successfully evaded, through either the distortion of dream or the rationalization of thought:

> That this is what we fear—no sight, no sound,
> No touch or taste or smell, nothing to think with,
> Nothing to love or link with,
> The anaesthetic from which none come round.[34]

Abandonment hardly poses the worst possible fate for a lover. More terrible is the inability to form any love relation at all because you are the one who is absent, you are the one not "here" or "anywhere." Behind every aubade, Larkin rightly intuits, lies a self-elegy, the Keatsian fear that "I may cease to be."

Not every solitary poet succumbs to this kind of anguished despair over nonbeing, and not every dawn song, it turns out, memorializes the departure of a lover. In an elegy to his steelworker father, Robert Gibb discovers at the end of his aubade that it is precisely in the existential void of dawn that he is closest to the person he loved most:

> Every day my father woke to a glare
> Like water breaking across his face,
> Bathed in the cold dawn of Pittsburgh,
> And walked away uphill. No music,
>
> No squares of sunshine unhinging themselves
> Like whole piazzas of heaven
> From the ceilings of Rome. Only the trolley
> Swaying beneath its grid of sky,

Surviving . . . Lovers

> The pigeons in Pittsburgh,
> Ringed and colored as oil slicks.[35]

The gritty workday dawn brings "no music" and "no squares of sunshine" to Gibb's blue-collar father, each day greeted not by larks in full song but by pigeons "ringed and colored as oil slicks." Yet the memory of his father's lonely uphill walk through grimy city streets is no longer, for the poet, a despairing one. Experiencing, years later, the same industrial dawn, Gibb awakens to the true nobility of his father's working-class existence: "this morning / Even my father walks with trumpets / Clear to the top of the hill." Dawn is not just the moment when we glimpse the possibility of our own deaths; it is also the time when the dead are most present to us, briefly recaptured in a state of semiconsciousness. Here the chief purpose of the aubade is to revive this precise moment of revival, as poetry directly taps into dawn's power to unleash remembrance.

Gibb's elegiac but exuberant dawn song poses a difficult question: Is the "requickening" power of the aubade strong enough to undo the tragic force of elegy? Or are aubade and elegy forever welded together—the desire for return simply the flip side of the reality of departure? What is perhaps most striking about the many modern aubades in which self and other have already been parted is that virtually none can imagine the other's return. They may long for it, even wait for it, but the return itself never happens. Gibb's aubade allows the poet to reexperience and reinterpret an early childhood memory of a father's dawn departure, yet it is a departure all the same; what is relived is the time the father went away, the Barthesian moment of parental abandonment. Even in this most determined of efforts to bring the dead back to life, the aubade itself invariably fails in the act of reanimation, which may be why the aubade will never outrun the elegy. In the race against time that marks both the aubade and the elegy, the poetry of loss will always surpass the poetry of love, for the simple reason that love itself is defined by loss. To paraphrase Barthes once again, love is the desire to be taken along. No waiting without departure, no passion without limits, no aubade without elegy.

surviving

But is there no way in which the aubade exceeds the elegy, no way in which love might overtake loss? When, or how, is an aubade not an elegy? Both aubades and elegies appear when the other is already gone; the beloved's absence is a necessary precondition for the writing of either an elegy or an aubade. And yet these poems differ radically in their tone. Ironically, the modern aubade—a verse form ostensibly dedicated to eros—is, by comparison, far less passionate than the majority of elegies discussed elsewhere in this book. Whereas most modern elegies appear as screams against the void, aubades emerge as gentle complaints, sad yet stoic acknowledgments of the death of passion. In the end, aubade poems, with all their radical investment in pleasure, are notably more realistic than elegies. More death drive than life drive, they operate less as testaments to the binding energies of love than as memorials to it.

Perhaps the greatest sign of the aubade's acquiescence to loss is its persistent avoidance of apostrophe. While some classic aubades, most especially the dialogue poems, invoke a "you" to restage the moment before parting, most modern aubades dispense with this rhetoric of revival altogether. The pronoun of choice in the aubade is not "you" but "I," with an occasional "he" or "she" actively resisting the revivifying powers of personification. For Barthes the beloved is a "who," for Pound a "she," for Samaras a "one," for Gibb a "my." When the "you" is directly invoked, in a poem like Wilbur's "A Late Aubade," it is in three continually shifting verb tenses (present, past, and future conditional), with no stable point of temporal orientation other than the interior thoughts of the speaking "I." Unlike the elegy, the aubade shows little pretense of being about, for, or to the other.

Surviving . . . Lovers

In the end, the main goal of the aubade is not revival but survival. Aubades testify not to the other's returning but to the subject's abiding, the ability to endure abandonment and live to tell the tale. In truth, there is something in the aubade that does not want the other back, at least not at the cost of displacing the self. Aubade poets intuit what elegists refuse to recognize: the possibility that the return of the absent beloved might represent not miraculous gain but renewed loss. In the economy of the aubade, losses only incur more losses, and the return of the other risks eclipsing or even killing the newly articulate self whose lyric voice depends entirely upon the other's absence. For the aubade poet, a poem represents not a substitute for a lost beloved so much as its own living entity, devoted solely to the continued existence of its author. "The death of the author" proves to be the clarion call only of elegies. Aubades have another purpose in mind: the survival of the author beyond the point of parting.

For the elegy, there is no possibility of the other's return; for the aubade, there is always the possibility of the other's return. And yet, in not a single aubade does the other ever *actually* return. It is as if the very threat of the beloved's return, the very real possibility that the beloved may come back to undo the lyric utterance, provokes the aubade poet to keep this reunion from ever happening. Instead, by eschewing the revivalist rhetoric of apostrophe and prosopopoeia, the poet captures and fixes the moment in time when the beloved is decidedly absent. While both elegy and aubade may ostensibly long for the return of the other, only the elegy takes pains to make it happen.

The tension between elegy and aubade is nowhere more powerfully articulated than in Elizabeth Bishop's "Aubade and Elegy," the only poem ever written to link these two powerful verse forms in its title. This anguished and arresting poem memorializes the rudest of all awakenings, the day Bishop woke to discover that her lover of fifteen years had taken an overdose of sedatives. As Lota de Macedo Soares lay in a coma, never to awaken, Bishop re-

Chapter Three

ports in shock to close friends: "sometime toward dawn she got up and tried to commit suicide—I heard her up in the kitchen about 6:30—she was already almost unconscious."[36] Bishop, who had recently left Brazil for New York (and it would appear Lota for Suzanne Bowen) struggled for years with the guilt she felt for not preventing the suicide.[37] Bishop could never bring herself to complete "Aubade and Elegy," her only self-proclaimed aubade and her only elegy for Lota. I cite here, in full, the only extant version of this manuscript poem:

> For perhaps the tenth time the tenth time the tenth time today
> and still early morning I go under the   crashing wave
> of ~~your~~ death
>
>   I go under the wave the black wave of ~~your~~ death
>
> ~~Your~~ e Not there! & not there! I see only small hands in the dirt
> transplanting sweet williams, tamping them down
> Dirt on ~~your~~ hands on ~~your~~ rings, ~~nothing more than that~~
>   but no more than that—
>
> No coffee can wake you no coffee can wake you no coffee
> No revolution can catch your attention
> You are bored with us all. It is true we ~~were~~ boring.
>
>   dark
> the smell of the earth, the smell of the ~~black~~ roasted coffee
> black as fine black as humus—
> no coffee can wake you no coffee can wake you no coffee can
>   wake you!
>   No coffee
>
> No coffee can wake you   no coffee can wake you no coffee
>   can wake you
>   No coffee[38]

Placed five times under erasure, Bishop's "your" renders painfully visible the profound tension between revival and survival,

Surviving . . . Lovers

between the elegy's desire to preserve the other and the aubade's need to save the self. Twice eliminating in stanza one the "your" before "death," the poem begins as a Larkin-like solitary aubade, portraying Bishop's repeated coming into consciousness of her own sure extinction. The elimination of the second-person possessive continues in stanza two, as the poet attempts to remove all traces of apostrophe, reducing her beloved to disembodied small hands transplanting flowers into dirt, an uncomfortable reprisal perhaps of Lota's Catholic burial, which Bishop never attended.[39] But what these opening stanzas labor to exclude, the poem's refrain brings back with a vengeance. "No coffee can wake you" resuscitates the "you" in the very act of insisting that she will never revive.

The allusion to coffee is far from incidental. Lota's gift to Bishop after arriving in New York was "12 kilo bags of coffee," a potent reminder of hundreds of shared mornings past, when the lovers woke each day to the smell of their favorite Brazilian beans. Going under the crashing wave of death for "the tenth time" also carried deep significance for Bishop, for the number ten, an apparent reference to the number of pills Lota took, was "the last word she said before going into a coma."[40] The incorporation of Lota's last word and last gift secure this poem's status as elegy. If there were any doubt, apostrophe, returning with the force of the repressed, quite nearly swamps the poem with the power of its pounding refrain: "no coffee can wake you no coffee can wake you no coffee can wake you." And yet this "you" may not refer exclusively to the beloved. What most startles about Bishop's "Aubade and Elegy" is how easily we can read the poem's proliferating second-person pronoun as a generic, self-referential "you." Two and a half years after Lota's death, Bishop may well be confessing her own emotional numbness, her late life depression fueled by alcohol and sedatives. For Bishop, every waking morning became a struggle with inertia, provoked by paralyzing terror of recurrent blackouts and the intimations of mortality they could not help but portend.

In the end, it is never clear in Bishop's "Aubade and Elegy" exactly whose death is being memorialized: the beloved's or the lover's. Barthes's structural dichotomy of "I" and "you," presence and absence, crumbles under the force of the title's conjunction ("and"), which holds both possibilities in place, presenting a poem that is at once elegy and aubade, revival and survival. Bishop's is the only poem I know to suggest that thanatos and eros may not be so different. Eros and thanatos, love and loss, occupy the same lyric space. It is tempting to conclude this book with the acknowledgment that nothing survives elegy. But Bishop's "Aubade and Elegy" hints that the aubade at least survives alongside the elegy. Mourning may conflate with morning for a reason. At the end of the day, waiting and waking are positions occupied by both mourners and lovers, making every ending a potential beginning and every elegy a possible aubade.

Who would I show it to

Conclusion

I began this book with W. S. Merwin's haunting elegy, a challenge to elegists and ethicists alike. With the beloved gone forever, and a world hell-bent on destroying itself, why bother to respond, act, write, or comfort? Consolation, it appears, has melted away in the conflagration of modernity, and ethics—the fundamental call to response—has died along with it. Or so we have come to believe.

But is this all there is to the story of dying modern? My meditation on elegy has sought to draw attention to surviving forms of elegy that refuse to fall entirely silent in the presence of modern death but instead persist in at least tentatively offering forms of emotional, political, or cultural response, even in the face of the most unimaginable of losses. It is the final claim of this book that it may be too soon to foreclose on consolation. Far from constituting an unethical response to mourning, poems that seek to acknowledge or redress loss continue to perform a vital function, reconstructing, repairing, and reinventing sundered lines of contact and communication.

The modern poetry of dying, reviving, and surviving all resuscitate the lost art of consolation, which in truth never really disappeared. Consolatory fictions live on, not despite modernity's melancholic rejection of aesthetic compensation but because of it. Deathbed poems, corpse poems, and aubades all demonstrate that the call to use language to maintain a meaningful if tenuous relation to those no longer present continues to speak to us. Consolation, in all three cases, resides in voice itself. Even the literary corpse poem, which so aggressively repudiates the fiction of a conscious afterlife, does so by deploying the voice of a speaking corpse. Voice, in the end, is all that remains. And it is poetic voice, I have argued, that puts the response back into responsibility.

Current critical thinking holds that it is only in the refusal of consolation that we find ethics; only by resisting an established literary mode like traditional elegy can a poet truly do justice to the unsettling and unsparing truth of dying modern. The reasoning is seductive enough: consolation elegies seek to sever our relation to the dead or absent other by incorporating the beloved in an act of mourning, while anti-elegies strive to honor the integrity of the dead by melancholically refusing the violence of interiorization. Anti-elegies turn against consolation in order not to destroy and not to forget, preserving the dead in all their radical alterity.

But taken together, the elegies I have addressed in this book compel me to ask whether it is true that anti-elegies are ethical and consolation elegies are unethical. The argument that underpins our prevailing notion of elegy is based on the common critical tendency to idealize or fetishize resistance; it assumes that only acts of melancholic refusal are ethical, while acts of hopeful reparation are not. But is reparation always an act of forgetting? And is refusal always an act of remembering? Can resistance, for resistance's sake, guarantee ethics? Are inherited models for writing about sudden or enduring grief ipso facto unethical, and can modernist despair truly be said to be the only real ethical response? Does it not matter what is being resisted or refused and when, how, and why? By the same token, does it not matter what is being reclaimed or restored?

As the examples in this book have illustrated, modern consolation poems are in fact quite diverse, their language, tenor, and tone notably dissimilar. Such diversity owes much to the way consolation itself in the modern period takes such complicated and contradictory forms. Consolation poems are not always naïve, just as anti-consolation poems are not always bitter. In the final analy-

Conclusion

sis, elegies cannot be so easily partitioned into the unethical or the ethical, in part because elegy articulates a fundamental paradox about ethics, the doleful yet hopeful refusal to give up on the other or, for that matter, the self. Even anti-elegies are, of course, elegies. Both typically share a concern for the departed, as well as for the survivor, though they may articulate these concerns differently. Stripped down to their most basic impulse, both the traditional consolation elegy and the modern anti-consolation elegy are answers to a call—responses to those beyond our reach, yet responses all the same.

But more than this, elegies are also themselves calls—attempts to restore the bonds of communication that the atrocities of modern death appear to have irreparably damaged. In the end, it is not clear whether these delicate lines of connection between self and other, lover and beloved, survivor and deceased have in fact been repaired, or whether the elegies themselves, often as richly allusive as they are deeply personal, have created their own community of mourners. But in both cases, it is the *effort* to restore or redress, the *desire* either to acknowledge those lost to us or to address those suffering like (or even instead of) us that powerfully articulates the ethical force at the heart of modern elegy. Like their predecessors, modern elegies are written to be read. I have learned over the course of writing this book that lurking behind every "who would I show it to" is a countervailing and compensatory truth: "Who *wouldn't* I show it to?"

I conclude not with Merwin's memorable maxim but with another equally resonant poetic anthem of midcentury American elegy, Randall Jarrell's "Can't you hear me?" In Jarrell's World War II poem "A Front," a group of bombers attempts to return to base as a severe weather front closes in. As five radio towers guide the bombers home, one bomber bounces to a secure landing while the others obey instructions to fly southward out of harm's way. Only one plane remains aloft, its broken radio transmitting but no longer receiving:

> The base is closed. . . . But one voice keeps on calling,
> The lowering pattern of the engines grows;
> The roar gropes downward in its shaky orbit
> For the lives the season quenches. Here below
> They beg, order, are not heard; and hear the darker
> Voice rising: *Can't you hear me? Over. Over—*
> All the air quivers, and the east sky glows.[1]

To transmit but no longer receive may constitute the defining moment of modern elegy. The poem ends tragically: the glowing east sky connotes not the promised resurrection of a brilliant rising sun but the fiery death of a horrific plane crash. "*Can't you hear me? Over. Over—*" are the pilot's actual last words, a desperate plea to be acknowledged, instructed, saved. For their part, the radio controllers "beg, order, are not heard." They hear the panicked "voice rising," but their own collective voices cannot reach the doomed pilot. To search and not find, to call and not be heard, these are recurrent themes in the era of dying modern, an age haunted by orphaned, abandoned, or lost voices. To Jarrell, the failure to be heard is its own kind of affront, and his elegy operates as a reproach to a violent world order in which the whole ethical system of call and response appears to be breaking down.

Elegy in the era of modern death is much like Jarrell's distress call: voices that keep calling for responses, despite the fear that none may be forthcoming. Elegies are voices without bodies, struggling hard, and against all odds, to make a connection. Continuing to demand a response, even when the channels of communication appear no longer operational, elegy offers not exercises in futility but lessons in responsibility. Elegy in general, and consolation elegy in particular, deserves a hearing in large part because it repeatedly acknowledges that before a call can be answered it must be fully heard. If modern elegists frequently ventriloquize the dead, they do so to keep the call alive, sending their own voices out into the wilderness with the conviction that while

Conclusion

not every voice makes it through, some do. In an age of unrelenting skepticism, not to say fatalism, elegy may be the one voice that keeps on calling.

Can't you hear me? Over. Over—

Notes

Introduction

1. Ariès, *The Hour of Our Death*, 405–6.
2. See, for example, Sacks, *The English Elegy*; Kay, *Melodious Tears*; Ramazani, *Poetry of Mourning*; Hammond, *The American Puritan Elegy*; Spargo, *The Ethics of Mourning*; Gilbert, *Death's Door*; Cavitch, *American Elegy*; and Breitwieser, *National Melancholy*.
3. Ramazani, *Poetry of Mourning*, xi. In his *Poetry of Mourning*, Ramazani provides the most persuasive reading of modern elegy as melancholic mourning. By employing the very phrase "melancholic mourning," Ramazani is careful not to oppose mourning and melancholia, allowing him to read modern elegy's "melancholic turn" (10) less as a break from traditional elegy than as an efflorescence of a tendency present in elegy from the beginning. My book perhaps comes closest in its focus to Spargo's *The Ethics of Mourning*, but here, too, Spargo's critical emphasis is on the melancholic or anti-elegiac—what he calls "a resistant or incomplete mourning" and sees as literature's greatest form of ethical protest (13). My own reading of modern elegy suggests that a refusal of consolation alone is not enough to guarantee ethics, just as consolation alone is not enough to rule it out.
4. I cite the evocative title of Zeiger's *Beyond Consolation*.
5. John B. Vickery deploys the phrase "the elegiac matrix" to describe the broadening focus of the modern elegy, which increasingly addresses many different types of losses: lives, loves, families, marriages, civilizations, cultures, philosophies, selves. Not all elegies, Vickery rightly reminds us, respond to the death of a person. See Vickery's *The Modern Elegiac Temper*, especially the introduction.
6. Preminger and Brogan, *The New Princeton Encyclopedia of Poetry and Poetics*, 322.

Notes to Chapter One

7. Alfred Lord Tennyson, *In Memoriam*, 121, 128. Max Cavitch locates, in the strong erotic investments of elegy, a larger truth defining genre as a whole: "genre is the way that eros manifests itself in the literary critical imagination" (personal correspondence with the author).

8. Spargo, *The Ethics of Mourning*, 8–9. In his most succinct formulation, Spargo locates "mournful agency at the heart of responsibility itself" (9).

9. See Johnson's "Using People: Kant with Winnicott" in her *Persons and Things*, 94–105.

10. Merwin, "Elegy," *The Second Four Books of Poems*, 226. For a lovely reading of Merwin's elegy as anti-elegy, see Scholes's *Semiotics and Interpretation*, 37–40.

Chapter 1.
Dying . . . Words

1. Day-Lewis, "Last Words," *The Complete Poems of C. Day Lewis*, 529–30.

2. See Jalland, *Death in the Victorian Family*, 26. Helen Burns's longing to return to her "last home," in Charlotte Brontë's *Jane Eyre*, provides one of the best-known examples of a good death in British fiction. On *Jane Eyre* as the "locus classicus" of Victorian deathbed literature, see Wheeler, *Death and the Future Life in Victorian Literature and Theology*, 38–39. Wheeler argues that "the last words of the dying . . . had a special significance for the Victorians, and became something of a literary convention in their own right" (30). The lingering passing of little Eva St. Clare in Harriet Beecher Stowe's *Uncle Tom's Cabin* provides the most famous American model of a virtuous death, designed in part to show that "some people die young in order to aid in the spiritual development of those whom they leave behind" (Romero, *Home*, 22). Romero further notes in her canny reading of Stowe's precocious consumptive that, in antebellum America, "a woman's dying gospel is perhaps even more potent than her living one" (22). For an interesting discussion of the cultural struggle to hold onto the notion of the good death and the convention of last words, even in the face of unprecedented carnage, see Faust's *This Republic of Suffering*, especially chapter one.

3. For exemplars of the perfect Christian death, Victorians turned back to the seventeenth century and to its flourishing literature of the *ars moriendi*. Already in its seventh American edition by 1836, Reverend Charles Drelincourt's 1651 French Protestant guide to dying well, titled

Notes to Chapter One

The Christian's Consolations against the Fear of Death, was a common bedside companion in nineteenth-century sickrooms. Intended in part to relieve the dying of the tremendous burden of last words, Drelincourt's deathbed manual offered prayers for every conceivable type of death, from dying as a king, general, or judge to dying young, on the battlefield, or in a foreign country.

4. Jalland, *Death in the Victorian Family*, 34–35.

5. The post-Enlightenment interest in last words is predominantly a Protestant tradition. In nineteenth-century Catholicism, last rites trumped last words as the necessary determinant of a good death. The Catholic deathbed accorded far greater authority to clergy than did the Evangelical deathbed, where the faith of the dying alone, rather than the power of priestly intervention, was believed to secure salvation. Subject even on the deathbed to the sacramental offices of the priest, Catholics appear to have had considerably less agency or responsibility for dying well, although Protestants, too, felt dependent on others—family especially—to help spiritually ready them for death. For more on the differences between Protestant and Catholic deathbeds in the nineteenth century, see Jalland, *Death in the Victorian Family*, 31–33. Ariès's monumental *The Hour of Our Death*, while aiming for full historical coverage, bases its account of Western deathbed rituals predominantly on Catholic deathbed traditions.

6. Maurice, *Sickness, Its Trials and Blessings, to which is appended Prayers for the Sick and Dying*, 322. Maurice at times appears troubled by the aggressive behavior of friends and family at the deathbed, eager to receive last words from the dying. She cautions deathbed attendants not to ask the loved one too many questions, not to literally prod or touch them, and not to say anything in the room they would not normally wish the sick person to hear, for "hearing is the sense that last goes, and first returns" (321–23). See also Tileston, *Sursum Corda*, 265–91. Most of the poems included in Tileston's "last hour" section are composed by women poets, including Alice Carey, Eliza Scudder, Dora Greenwell, and Elizabeth Charles. As primary attendants in the sickroom, women witnessed many a deathbed scene and frequently wrote about what they saw. Lydia Sigourney, for one, devotes an entire memoir, and many poems, to the short life and dying words of her nineteen-year-old son, Andrew. An aspiring writer who died a lingering death from tuberculosis in 1850, Andrew wound his watch and notified his family and friends that "at twelve o'clock, I shall be gone" (Sigourney, *The Faded Hour*, 235).

7. J. C. Sharp briefly summarizes for his Victorian readers John

Notes to Chapter One

Keble's theory of prosody in the preface to Keble's *The Christian Year*. Keble, who held the Oxford Chair of Poetry from 1831 to 1841, affirms that "high and tender feeling controlled and modified by a certain reserve is the very soul of poetry" (Sharp, preface, vii). For a fuller introduction to Keble's thoughts on prosody, see *Keble's Lectures on Poetry, 1832–1841*. Wheeler, in his *Death and the Future Life in Victorian Literature and Theology*, notes the importance of Keble's widely reprinted verse volume (57), while Jalland further observes, in her *Death in the Victorian Family*, that Keble's devotional book of poems maintained its immense popularity even against such formidable challengers as Alfred Lord Tennyson's *In Memoriam* (281–83).

8. Sigourney, *The Weeping Willow*, v.

9. Emily Dickinson is especially fond of the trope of the "dying eye," which appears most prominently in the poems "I've seen a Dying Eye" (P, 648), "Dying! To be afraid of them" (946), and "Robbed by Death—but that was easy" (838). For the Dickinson poems discussed in this book, I follow the chronology and numbering employed in R. W. Franklin's edition of *The Poems of Emily Dickinson*, hereafter cited within the text as *P*.

10. Ware, "Seasons of Prayer," in Cheever, *The American Commonplace Book of Poetry*, 143–44.

11. Nancy Lee Beaty, in *The Craft of Dying*, argues that of all the helpful offices which bystanders could perform at the deathbed—including providing a crucifix and holy water or persuading the sick that there is little time to waste—prayer on behalf of the dying was considered by devotional literature as the most important role of the witness (29).

12. Westwood, "Last Words," *Poems*, 171.

13. See Vendler, *Invisible Listeners*.

14. Jackson, "Last Words," *Poems*, 173.

15. See Seeman, *Pious Persuasions*. Last words, Seeman notes, transformed "ordinarily marginalized female speech into the center of male and clerical attention" (75). Clergy and laity also viewed last words quite differently: "ministers argued that they demonstrated the *possibility* that a person was saved, while most laypeople regarded them as *proof* that a person was saved" (65).

16. Jackson's own last wishes (which included her strong desire that her husband marry her niece) were in fact fulfilled. The rustic grave on Cheyenne Mountain, the plain granite tombstone, and the simple funeral proceedings all accorded with the directions Jackson enumer-

Notes to Chapter One

ates in her poem "Last Words," read aloud at the gravesite per the poet's request. See Phillips, *Helen Hunt Jackson*, 271–74.

17. Sigourney, "Last Words of an Indian Chief," *Pocahontas, and Other Poems*, 181–82.

18. Sigourney, *Letters to Young Ladies*, 327. For a brief discussion of all three traditions, see Murray, *Forked Tongues*, especially 34–37. On the dying Indian speech, see also Bross, "Dying Saints, Vanishing Savages"; and Seeman, "Reading Indians' Deathbed Scenes."

19. Of greater concern than even how one is buried is the more troubling question of with whom. The "bury me/bury me not" lyrics may well be the most political poems in nineteenth-century literature, for in an era when the dead were believed to live in their tombs, nothing incited public passions more than the (mis)treatment of dead bodies.

20. Harper, "Bury Me in a Free Land," n.p. This pre-Civil War poem sees the land itself as so contaminated by the blood of slavery as to be unfit for human burial. Yet, in "Sacred Land Regained," Donald Yacovone convincingly argues that the 1858 "Bury Me in a Free Land," with its strong dismissal of a nation's soil poisoned by the blood of the lash, needs to be read in relation to a later 1863 poem memorializing the first army unit of free blacks, whose fight against slavery during the Civil War now transformed and redeemed the American land through blood voluntarily shed.

21. Wolosky, *Major Voices*, 159. This useful anthology includes Harper's poem on pages 163–64.

22. Scholars disagree on whether or not Dickinson attended more than one deathwatch, her mother's in 1882 (just four years before the poet's own passing). The poet was, however, abundantly familiar with the Evangelical literature on the subject.

23. See Phelps, *The Still Hour*.

24. See Pound, *American Ballads and Songs*, xxii. Perhaps best remembered today as one of Willa Cather's college classmates and early love interest, Louise Pound had a distinguished career of her own, as a folklorist, professor, and the first woman president of the Modern Language Association. For more examples of the American murder ballad, see Burt, *American Murder Ballads and Their Stories*; and Lomax and Lomax, *American Ballads and Folk Ballads*.

25. "Johnny Randall," in Pound, *American Ballads and Songs*, 3.

26. "The Cruel Brother," in Pound, *American Ballads and Songs*, 23.

27. "The Jealous Lover," in Pound, *American Ballads and Songs*, 101–2.

Notes to Chapter One

28. Cooke, "Faithful," *Poems*, 236–38.
29. Ibid., 236.
30. After Othello strangles his wife in a jealous rage, the innocent Desdemona later revives long enough to improbably claim that she herself has done the deed. For more on Desdemona's "loving lie" or "false confession," see Guthke's *Last Words*, 43–45. Although Guthke devotes no more than a paragraph to the poetry of last words, this book nonetheless offers a useful and entertaining introduction to the history of last words, spanning from the medieval period to the end of the twentieth century.
31. "Wicked Polly," in Pound, *American Ballads and Songs*, 113, 112, 113.
32. Guthke devotes an entire chapter of his *Last Words* to "Guidance, Entertainment, and Frisson: Anthologies of Last Words," 98–154.
33. Burns, "The Death and Dying Words of Poor Mailie, The Author's Only Pet Yowe: An Unco Mournfu' Tale," *The Complete Poetical Works of Robert Burns*, 14–15.
34. Robertson, "The Last Speech and Dying Words of Willy, a Pet-Lamb, who was executed by the Hands of a common Butcher, for gnawing, tearing, and murdering one of Miss ——— lac'd Ruffles," *Poems on Several Occasions*, 126, 127, 126. For a more recent example of the genre, see Hesketh's "Animals' Last Words," *The Leave Train*, 144.
35. Robertson, "The Last Speech and Dying Words of Willy, a Pet-Lamb, who was executed by the Hands of a common Butcher, for gnawing, tearing, and murdering one of Miss ——— lac'd Ruffles," *Poems on Several Occasions*, 127.
36. Dylan Thomas, "Do Not Go Gentle into that Good Night," *The Poems of Dylan Thomas*, 239. Thomas wrote this now famous villanelle for his father, but at first he circulated it only to friends, unconvinced his father was aware he was dying.
37. Gilbert, *Inventions of Farewell*, 35. Gilbert describes the tragic death of her husband, just hours after routine surgery, in her memoir *Wrongful Death*, and no less movingly in her ambitious scholarly study *Death's Door*. All three books, Gilbert suggests, have been attempts to claim her grief "at a historical moment when death was in some sense unspeakable" (*Death's Door*, xix).
38. On the bureaucratization of death in the twentieth century, see Ramazani's *Poetry of Mourning*. Ramazani locates the modern desire to impose order and discipline on dying "not only in such three-dimensional spaces as the funeral parlor, the cemetery, the hos-

Notes to Chapter One

pital, the war monument, and the columbarium, but also in such two-dimensional spaces as the newspaper, television, and film" (18).

39. Rich, "The Parting: II," *Collected Early Poems*, 274.

40. Moulton, "The Last Good-by," *In the Garden of Dreams*, 81.

41. Moulton herself, after a long illness, died peacefully in her sleep. According to an account provided by friend and fellow writer Harriet Prescott Spofford, Moulton died "unaware of the immanence of death" and "crossed into that unknown without suffering or recognition of it" (Spofford, introduction to *The Poems and Sonnets of Louise Chandler Moulton*, xix).

42. Millay, "Interim," *Collected Poems*, 14–24.

43. See Flanders's chapter on the sickroom in her *Inside the Victorian Home*, 340–89. Flanders explains that "it was recommended that, at the commencement of illness, the sickroom be emptied as much as possible of all furniture and ornaments. In the second half of the century, disease theory indicated that bare, spare rooms were more conducive to patients' recovery" (353).

44. Williams, "Last Words of My English Grandmother," *The Collected Poems of William Carlos Williams*, 464–65.

45. There are two versions of Williams's poem, with the slightly altered titles "Last Words of My Grandmother" and "Last Words of My English Grandmother." I have quoted from the latter; the former—the earlier poem—also appears in *The Collected Poems of William Carlos Williams*, 253–55. The poem's early incarnation provides the narrative context missing from the second and shorter version. In the first version, Williams carefully chronicles the time, place, and progression of his grandmother's dementia, from the moment she takes ill to her dying words in the ambulance. Adopting a voice oddly distanced from the events described, the poet initially speaks of his grandmother as "the old lady," "an old woman," or "the dazed old woman," while describing himself as "the boy" or "the young grandson, nineteen / whom she had raised." In the poem's final streamlined revision, Williams drops the third-person voice, omits the lengthy narrative exposition, and elects to begin inside the sickroom, on the morning of his grandmother's death. These extensive changes shift the poem's emotional tone from impersonal to personal and its narrative tenor from story to memory, all the while refocusing the poem around the grandmother's last words proper.

46. Dennis, "Arthur from the Barge," 30.

47. Gunn, "Lament," *The Man with Night Sweats*, 63.

Notes to Chapter One

48. Johnson, "Last Words," *Aid and Comfort*, 8.

49. Mary Catharine O'Connor, *The Art of Dying Well*. O'Connor rejects the common wisdom that the *Ars moriendi* were written for clergy as manuals for ministering to the sick; the emergence of epidemics in the late medieval period, she argues, necessitated that Christians "be given a method of directing their own passing to a happy eternity" (7). For more on the history of the *Ars moriendi*, see White, *English Devotional Literature*; and Beaty, *The Craft of Dying*.

50. O'Connor, *The Art of Dying Well*, 8.

51. Monette, "No Goodbyes," *Love Alone*, 4–5. In Monette's book of elegies, composed in the five months following Roger Horwitz's death, warfare imagery permeates even the book's short preface. Writing from "the front lines," the poet explains that he writes of "only one man's passing and one man's cry, a warrior burying a warrior" (xiii). Monette, who himself died of AIDS in 1995, provides a prose account of Horwitz's death in one of the first published AIDS memoirs, *Borrowed Time*.

52. In *The Gift of Death*, Jacques Derrida writes that "death is very much that which nobody else can undergo or confront in my place," adding that "no one can die for me if 'for me' means instead of me, in my place" (41).

53. See Zeiger, *Beyond Consolation*, 108.

54. Dunn, "Thirteen Steps and the Thirteenth of March," *Elegies*, 13–14.

55. Ibid., 14.

56. Hall, *Without*, especially "Last Days," 35–45.

57. Dana Levin, "The Heroics of Style," 45. For more on modernism's famous dictum, see Ezra Pound's *Make It New*.

58. Reverend Charles Drelincourt is surely the best case in point. The churchman's death in 1669 from apoplexy, recounted in the preface to *The Christian's Consolations against the Fear of Death*, offered readers an inspirational model of proper deathbed decorum. Despite a racking cough and raging fever, Drelincourt managed in his final hours to summon friends and family, recommend his family's care to his son-in-law, settle his domestic affairs, plan his church service, instruct his children to live in perfect union, reward his deathbed attendants, bless his children, and "glorify God to the last gasp." Drelincourt requested that his own "Consolation Prayer for a Dying Minister" be read back to him in his dying hour, demonstrating that this famous minister of the Reformed Church of Paris, who had spent a lifetime instructing others in a holy death, was nothing if not prepared for his own (v–xxiv).

Notes to Chapter One

59. Antler, "Last Words," *Last Words*, 13–14.
60. The text most responsible for canonizing "more light!" as Goethe's dying declaration would appear to be Lewes's *The Life of Goethe*, 559. For more on the fascinating genealogy of the German poet's apocryphal last words, see Guthke, *Last Words*, 81–89.
61. Rilke, *Duino Elegies & Sonnets to Orpheus*, 51.
62. Sexton, "Love Letter Written in a Burning Building," *The Complete Poems*, 613–15, 614.
63. See Durrell, "A Patch of Dust," *Collected Poems*, 337–38; Roethke, "Last Words," *The Collected Poems of Theodore Roethke*, 48; and Pastan, "Last Words," *A Fraction of Darkness*, 42. The quotation is from David Ray, "Mehr Licht," *Demons in the Diner*, 75–78. See also Sexton, "Hurry Up Please It's Time," *The Death Notebooks*, 62–74.
64. Douglas, *The Feminization of American Culture*, 206.
65. Sigourney, *Letters of Life*, 408–13.
66. McIntyre, *Dirt & Diety*, 398. Burns's death has been variously attributed to alcoholism, syphilis, rheumatism, lupus, hepatitis, leukemia, tuberculosis, brucellosis, pneumonia, or lead poisoning (McIntyre, *Dirt & Diety*, 431–33).
67. Sean Day-Lewis, *C. Day-Lewis*. Sean Day-Lewis's disappointment over the banality of the deathbed farewell is undisguised: "I felt we should have said profound things to one another" (304).
68. Milford, *Savage Beauty*, 508.
69. Stevenson, *Bitter Fame*, 298–99; Axelrod, *Sylvia Plath*, 218.
70. Middlebrook, *Anne Sexton*, 396–97, 107. For a more extended discussion of the problem the convention of last words poses for biographers, who are not above cleverly staging for their subjects an edifying or exemplary death, see Lee's entertaining "How to End It All," chapter 4 of her *Virginia Woolf's Nose*, 95–122.
71. See Clark, "The Last Words of Hart Crane as He Becomes One with the Gulf," *Fractured Karma*, 86.
72. Derrida, *The Work of Mourning*, 45.
73. Quoted in Lockyer, *Last Words of Saints and Sinners*, 9.
74. Blanchot, *The Space of Literature*, 38, 44, 54.
75. For example, of the four poems cited above on Goethe's last words, one uses "more light" as a title (Ray), another foregrounds them in the opening stanza (Pastan), while still another locates them in the exact center of the poem (Durrell). Only Roethke chooses to place an oblique reference to Goethe's last words in the poem's concluding verse, though in the beginning, and not the end, of the line.

Notes to Chapter Two

76. In *Poetic Closure*, Barbara Herrnstein Smith attributes the stylistic pluralism of modern poetry, and its preference for open-ended closure, to the modern suspicion that "all last words are lies" (241).

77. James Richardson, aphorism 149, *Interglacial*, 226.

Chapter 2.
Reviving . . . Corpses

1. Fried, "Repetition, Refrain, and Epitaph," 615.

2. For more on the epitaph, see Mills-Court, *Poetry as Epitaph*; Chase, "Reading Epitaphs"; Edgette, "The Epitaph and Personality Revelation"; Petrino, "'Alabaster Chambers': Dickinson, Epitaphs, and the Culture of Mourning," in her *Emily Dickinson and Her Contemporaries*, 96–128; and Fry, "The Absent Dead."

3. For a useful critique of Philippe Ariès's "denial of death" thesis, see Jonathan Dollimore's *Death, Desire and Loss in Western Culture*. Dollimore notes that Foucault's rejection of the repressive hypothesis on sex might pertain to death as well. Like talk of sex in the nineteenth century, talk of death during the same period was not "repressed so much as resignified," producing "a never-ending analysis of it" (126).

4. Literary history provides examples of speaking corpses before the nineteenth century, though these corpses are fewer in number and in kind. Early modern corpse poems, often epitaphs in the manner of Robert Herrick's "On Himselfe" or Ben Jonson's epitaph on Sir Charles Cavendish, dramatize "the movement from personal grief to public praise," in the words of Joshua Scodel (*The English Poetic Epitaph*, 9). In contrast, nineteenth- and twentieth-century corpse poems (as this chapter suggests) abjure both personal grief and public praise, reaching beyond a poetics of mourning. In a kind of literary relay, the decline of the epitaph in the romantic period (Scodel, *The English Poetic Epitaph*, 344–407) gives way to the first real stirrings of the modern corpse poem, a form of mortuary verse that largely dispenses with older conventions of memorialization. For discussions of the corpse in the early modern period, see Gittings, *Death, Burial and the Individual in Early Modern England*; and D. Vance Smith, *Arts of Dying* (manuscript in progress).

5. Wolfson and Manning, *Selected Poems of Hood, Praed and Beddoes*, 33–34.

6. Wolfson and Manning note that in "Mary's Ghost" Hood's "punning dispersal of the female body literalizes with ghoulish comedy the

Notes to Chapter Two

Renaissance trope of the *blason*" (*Selected Poems of Hood, Praed and Beddoes*, 324).

7. Hardy, "Ah, Are You Digging on my Grave?" *The Complete Poems of Thomas Hardy*, 330–31.

8. See Ruth Richardson's fascinating *Death, Dissection, and the Destitute*. Richardson argues that the Anatomy Act, far from protecting the poor, made them more vulnerable to the threat of medical dissection, legally expanding the pool of available corpses from hanged murderers to anyone who died a pauper.

9. Freud, *Totem and Taboo*, in *The Standard Edition* 13: 57–67.

10. Richardson, *Death, Dissection, and the Destitute*, 15. See also Werner, *The Formation of Christian Dogma*, especially chapter 11.

11. Dickinson composed three general types of corpse poems: poems spoken about corpses, poems spoken by corpses, and poems in which it is simply impossible to tell which side of the grave the speaker is on. Of these seventy or so poems, at least a third are clearly identifiable as corpse poems in the manner I have described: poems spoken from the point of view of the deceased.

12. Donne, "Death be not proud" (Holy Sonnet 6), *John Donne*, 176.

13. In those speaking corpse poems where no feminine pronouns are used and no clues to the speaker's gender are provided, Dickinson presents the body as neither male nor female but as simply a body without a clearly demarcated gender. Although Dickinson elsewhere assumes male voices, her avoidance of a distinctly male persona in the corpse poems can perhaps be explained by the poet's close identification with her subject, so close that it may in fact be herself she envisions finally in the grave. The poet may also have viewed it as entirely unseemly to inhabit a male cadaver.

14. Hallam Tennyson, *Alfred Lord Tennyson*, 396.

15. Alfred Lord Tennyson, "Maud," *Tennyson's Poetry*, 244.

16. Grigson, "A Sandy Burial," *A Skull in Salop and Other Poems*, 47.

17. Grigson, "Epitaph," *Collected Poems, 1963–1980*, 188.

18. Jacobs, "The Dying of Death," 265, 264.

19. Verdery, *The Political Lives of Dead Bodies*, chapter 1.

20. Hughes, "Ballads of Lenin," *The Collected Poems of Langston Hughes*, 183–84.

21. Richard Wright, "Between the World and Me," in Forché, *Against Forgetting*, 633–34.

22. Kristeva, *Powers of Horror*, 4.

Notes to Chapter Two

23. The depersonalization of the human cadaver from the nineteenth to the twentieth century is a complex and often contradictory movement that may, in the end, describe historical perception more than historical fact. The figure of the anonymous corpse, indistinguishable on the battlefield, can already be identified in representations of the Civil War dead, while the figure of the beloved corpse, washed and waked at home, can still be found in representations of the modern dead. For more on the social history of death, see Kselman, *Death and the Afterlife in Modern France*; Quigley, *The Corpse*; Laderman, *The Sacred Remains*; Sloane, *The Last Great Necessity*; Ruby, *Secure the Shadow*; and Farrell, *Inventing the American Way of Death*.

24. Eliot, *The Waste Land*, in *T. S. Eliot*, 39. Michael H. Levenson reads this entire opening section of *The Waste Land* as narrated by a corpse, "a corpse that has not yet died" (*Geneology of Modernism*, 172).

25. Jarrell, "The Death of the Ball Turret Gunner," *The Complete Poems*, 144.

26. Jarrell, "Losses," *Little Friend, Little Friend*, 15–16.

27. Borowski, "Farewell to Maria," *Tadeusz Borowski*, 110–13; Celan, "Psalm," *Selected Poems and Prose of Paul Celan*, 157. Borowski and Celan, survivors of the camps, both later committed suicide. I have found speaking corpses in poems of survivors who did not commit suicide, but, strikingly, virtually none in the work of those who did.

28. Langer, *Art from the Ashes*, 555.

29. Jacob Glatstein, "I Have Never Been Here Before," in Langer, *Art from the Ashes*, 658–59.

30. Delbo, *Auschwitz and After*, 267. On the paradox of trauma and survival, see Caruth, *Unclaimed Experience*; and Dori Laub's clinical contributions to Felman and Laub, *Testimony*, 57–92. Susan Brison, who cites the Delbo quote as an epigraph, offers the phrase "outliving oneself" to describe the peculiar experience of surviving one's own death ("Outliving Oneself: Trauma, Memory, and Personal Identity," 12–39).

31. Yevgeny Yevtushenko, "Babii Yar," in Schiff, *Holocaust Poetry*, 94.

32. Pagis, "An Opening to Satan," *The Selected Poetry of Dan Pagis*, 30.

33. Other corpse poems by Pagis include "Siege," "Testimony," and "Footprints," all of which can be found in *The Selected Poetry of Dan Pagis*.

34. On apostrophe, see Johnson, "Apostrophe, Animation, and Abortion," *A World of Difference*, 184–99; and Culler, "Apostrophe," *The Pursuit of Signs*, chapter seven.

Notes to Chapter Two

35. Wordsworth, "Essays upon Epitaphs," *The Prose Works of William Wordsworth*, 60; de Man, "Hypogram and Inscription, Michael Riffaterre's Poetics of Reading," 33.

36. Deconstructive essays on the trope of prosopopoeia all cite the same lines from Paul de Man's "Autobiography and Displacement," singling out for attention de Man's remark on "the latent threat that inhabits prosopopoeia, namely that by making the death [sic] speak, . . . the living are struck dumb, frozen in their own death" (*The Rhetoric of Romanticism*, 78). These essays resuscitate de Man by speaking as de Man, through the vehicle of citationality. Deconstructive treatments of prosopopoeia are all prosopopoeic acts, attempts at reanimation in which the dead figure who is repeatedly made to speak is the figure of Paul de Man. See, for example, Derrida, *Memoires for Paul de*; Riffaterre, "Prosopopeia"; and Zeiger, *Beyond Consolation*. For more on the critical and literary history of prosopopoeia, see Paxson, *The Poetics of Personification*.

37. Payne, "Resurrection," *The Way of the Winepress*, 21–22.

38. Fuller, "Ghost Voice," *New and Collected Poems*, 436–38.

39. Davison, "Eurydice in Darkness," *The Poems of Peter Davison*, 64; Hadas, "Eurydice," *Designing Women*, 78.

40. H. D., "Eurydice," *H. D. Collected Poems*, 51–55.

41. Bishop, "One Art," *Elizabeth Bishop: The Complete Poems*, 178.

42. Ramazani, commenting on Bishop's "One Art," suggests "if the traditional elegy was an art of saving, the modern elegy is . . . an art of losing" (*Poetry of Mourning*, 4). While the literary corpse poem explicitly challenges the commemorative powers of elegy, many poets (Thomas Hardy perhaps chief among them) write both elegies *and* corpse poems, effectively hedging their bets.

43. See, respectively, Miranda's "Icarus" from "Triptych," *Listeners at the Breathing Place*, 19; Holmes's "Chez Persephone," *The Physicist at the Mall*, 16–17; Pagis's "Autobiography," *The Selected Poetry of Dan Pagis*, 5–6; Plath's "Lady Lazarus," *The Collected Poems of Sylvia Plath*, 244–47; Rich's "Phantasia for Elvira Shatayev," *The Dream of a Common Language*, 4–6; Alfred Corn's "And Then I Saw," in Gibson, *Blood & Tears*, 30–31; Phelps's "Absent!" *Songs of the Silent World*, 20–22; and Masters's *Spoon River Anthology*.

44. Yeats, "The Circus Animals' Desertion," *The Collected Poems of W. B. Yeats*, 348.

45. Agamben, *The End of the Poem*, 74.

Notes to Chapter Three

46. Derrida, "Signature Event Context," *Limited Inc*, 1–23; Barthes, "The Death of the Author," *The Rustle of Language*, 49–55.

47. Celan, "Nocturnally Pursed," *Selected Poems and Prose of Paul Celan*, 69.

48. Plath, "Stillborn," *The Collected Poems of Sylvia Plath*, 142.

Chapter 3.
Surviving . . . Lovers

1. I am reminded of Elizabeth Bishop's autobiographical story "In the Village," in which the poet's childhood self, overhearing a discussion of mourning clothes, simply cannot fathom why one must wear black in the morning. See Bishop, *Elizabeth Bishop: The Collected Prose*, 254.

2. I cite the translation from Arthur T. Hatto's impressively researched edited volume *Eos: An Enquiry into the Theme of Lovers' Meetings and Partings at Dawn in Poetry*, 371–72. This volume, collated in the 1950s, records dawn songs from fifty different languages, including Arabic, Russian, Thai, Hungarian, Persian, and Japanese. The Old French aubade I cite here is tentatively attributed to the famous French songwriter Gace Brulé and is clearly influenced by the troubadours.

3. For more on the dawn song as an "expressive plaint" that serves as love's "final issue," see Sigal, *Erotic Dawn-Song of the Middle Ages*, 1.

4. This is not to say that aubades never deploy meter. Some do, though (unlike a sonnet or a villanelle, for example) they refuse to mark time in any standardized, generic, or regularized form. The aubade lover seeks to occupy a space where time stands still.

5. Saville, *The Medieval Erotic Alba*, 238. Despite the sheer volume of modern aubades (especially compared to their medieval predecessors), there has been no attention paid to these poems as a whole, with the possible exception of an enchanting essay by Edward Hirsch, "The Work of Lyric: Night and Day." In a short section on the dawn song, Hirsh wonders if the aubade, moving as it does from darkness to light, silence to speech, might in fact operate as "one of the quintessential forms of lyric" (371).

6. See Old Provençal aubades nos. 7 and 4 in Hatto, *Eos*, 365–66, 362–63.

7. As T. J. B. Spencer notes, in the English, Scottish, Anglo-Irish, and American traditions, aubades and albas largely disappear between the mid-seventeenth century and the mid-nineteenth century, though he

Notes to Chapter Three

does not explain why (see Hatto, *Eos*, 529). It is possible that this secular medieval form, uninfluenced by Greek or Roman literature, was less attractive to poets of the neoclassical eighteenth century. In the romantic period, a case can be made I think for reading John Keats's "La Belle Dame Sans Merci" (1819) as an aubade. Borrowing his title from a late medieval poem, Keats's balladeer sings of a knight at arms with a lily on his dew-covered brow, discovered "alone and palely loitering" after a night spent in thrall to a beautiful lady who abandoned him in the morning. Renewed literary interest in the aubade appears to take hold in the late Victorian period, as scholars begin to make a serious study of the medieval aubade and its various types and origins (see Hatto, *Eos*, 21).

8. Barthes, *A Lover's Discourse: Fragments*, 13; hereafter cited within the text as ALD. More poem than treatise, Barthes's lexicon of love explicitly seeks "to stage an utterance, not an analysis" (3).

9. See also Cavitch's economical and eloquent definition of elegy: "elegies are poems about being left behind" (*American Elegy*, 1).

10. Curiously, Howard's English translation of *A Lover's Discourse* omits altogether the second of Barthes's three aubades, as if weary of Barthes's endless complaint. I cite here the original French version with my own translation for the second aubade.

11. Whitman, "When Lilacs Last in the Dooryard Bloomed," *Leaves of Grass and Other Writings*, 276–83. The picked lilac, prematurely broken, may be the most resonant elegiac image in American literature, at once moving tribute and violent token.

12. I reference here the title to Jacques Lacan's 1936 paper, "Beyond the 'Reality Principle,'" *Écrits*, 58–74.

13. Stevie Smith, "Aubade," *Collected Poems*, 46.

14. Ibid.

15. Yeats, "Parting," *The Collected Poems of W. B. Yeats*, 233.

16. Browning, "Meeting at Night" and "Parting at Morning," *Robert Browning, Selected Poems*, 43.

17. Swinburne, "Before Parting," *Poems and Ballads*, 209–10. Other Swinburne aubades include "In the Orchard" (113–15) and "Before Dawn" (171–74).

18. Swinburne, "Before Parting," *Poems and Ballads*, 209–10.

19. For Barthes on corruption and defascination, see "Un petit point du nez" (The tip of the nose), in the original French version of *Fragments d'un discourse amoureux*, 33.

Notes to Chapter Three

20. Ezra Pound, "Alba," *Lustra of Ezra Pound*, 51.

21. Although early aubades may include Christian symbolism, the form tends to be not anti-Christian so much as non-Christian (see Saville, *The Medieval Erotic Alba*, 102). Aubades celebrate secular love, privileging eros over faith, passion over piety.

22. Sylvia Plath, in a series of meditations on pregnancy, birth, and barrenness, finds in the departing lover aubade a powerful vehicle for articulating her own deeply mixed feelings about motherhood. Poems like "Morning Song," "Barren Women," and "Heavy Women," all composed within the same week shortly after the birth of Plath's son, Nicholas, together invoke classic aubade motifs (night, day, dawn, white, flowers, windows, sleeping, waking) to explore birthing as a form of uncoupling. In Plath, the departing lover poem becomes the departing mother poem. See Plath, *Collected Poems: Sylvia Plath*, 156–58.

23. Shapiro, "Aubade," *Collected Poems*, 271–72.

24. Orr, "Aubade," *City of Salt*, 42.

25. Samaras, "Aubade: Macedonia," *Hands of the Saddlemaker*, 21–22.

26. Shapiro, "Aubade," *Selected Poems*, 93. See also Parker's "Aubade: The Hotel Cleveland," 227.

27. Worley, "Sunday Aubade," 38–39.

28. Crapsey, "Aubade," *The Complete Poems and Collected Letters of Adelaide Crapsey*, 114.

29. Wilbur, "A Late Aubade," *Collected Poems*, 229–30. Other aubades featuring lovers who elect to remain in bed include G. S. Fraser's "Aubade," *Poems of G. S. Fraser*, 120–21; and Louise Glück's "Aubade," *Descending Figure*, 38.

30. Wilbur, "A Late Aubade," *Collected Poems*, 229–30.

31. Payne, "Aubade," *The Poetical Works of John Payne*, 238–40.

32. Larkin, "Aubade," *Collected Poems*, 190–91.

33. Freud, "Thoughts on War and Death" (1915), *The Standard Edition* 14: 289.

34. Larkin, "Aubade," *Collected Poems*, 190–91.

35. Gibb, "Aubade," *The Origins of Evening*, 105–6.

36. Elizabeth Bishop to U. T. and Joseph Summers, September 23, 1967, in Bishop, *One Art*, 468.

37. Bishop struggled, unsuccessfully, to absolve herself of guilt for not seeing Lota's secret intentions the afternoon she arrived in New York: "Why did I sleep so soundly?—why why why—I can't help thinking I might have saved her somehow—gone over and over that Sunday

Notes to Conclusion

afternoon but honestly can't think of anything I did especially wrong—except that I have done many things wrong all my life" (letter to U. T. and Joseph Summers, September 28, 1967, in Bishop, *One Art*, 470). For more on Bishop's affairs at this time with not one but two artists' wives, Lilli Correia de Araújo and Suzanne Bowen, see Millier, *Elizabeth Bishop*, 368–70, 378–84.

38. Bishop, "Aubade and Elegy," *Edgar Allan Poe & the Juke-Box*, 149.

39. In her notebook preparations for this poem, Bishop lists more than two dozen of Lota's memorable qualities suitable for elegizing, among them her elegance, snobbery, superiority, temper, heroism, sadness, piety, anger, humor, and courage. Yet Bishop soon enough abandons elegy's traditional litany of character traits to consider instead how Lota's death has changed forever the very fabric of once-tranquil mornings—"the beautiful light of morning," a "theatre full of blue metallic birds," "mountains shouldering each other / away from the sun," and "the poor cats come for our breakfast," attracted by the smell of coffee "as fine as fine humus as black." See Bishop, *Edgar Allan Poe & the Juke-Box*, 220.

40. Elizabeth Bishop to Maria Osser, October 2, 1967, in Bishop, *One Art*, 471.

Conclusion

1. Jarrell, "A Front," *Randall Jarrell, The Complete Poems*, 173.

Bibliography

Agamben, Giorgio. *The End of the Poem: Studies in Poetics*. Translated by Daniel Heller-Roazen. Stanford: Stanford University Press, 1999.
Antler. *Last Words*. New York: Ballantine, 1986.
Ariès, Philippe. *The Hour of Our Death: The Classic History of Western Attitudes toward Death Over the Last One Thousand Years*. Translated by Helen Weaver. New York: Alfred A. Knopf, 1981.
Axelrod, Steven Gould. *Sylvia Plath: The Wound and the Cure of Words*. Baltimore: Johns Hopkins University Press, 1990.
Barthes, Roland. *Fragments d'un discourse amoureux*. Paris: Éditions du Seuil, 1977.
———. *A Lover's Discourse: Fragments*. New York: Hill and Wang, 1978.
———. *The Rustle of Language*. Translated by Richard Howard. Berkeley: University of California Press, 1989.
Beaty, Nancy Lee. *The Craft of Dying: A Study in the Literary Tradition of the* Ars moriendi *in England*. New Haven: Yale University Press, 1970.
Bishop, Elizabeth. *Edgar Allan Poe & the Juke-Box*. Edited by Alice Quinn. New York: Farrar, Straus and Giroux, 2006.
———. *Elizabeth Bishop: The Collected Prose*. New York: Farrar, Straus and Giroux, 1984.
———. *Elizabeth Bishop: The Complete Poems, 1927–1979*. New York: Noonday Press, 1992.
———. *One Art: Letters*. Edited by Robert Giroux. New York: Farrar, Straus and Giroux, 1994.
Blanchot, Maurice. *The Space of Literature*. Translated by Ann Smock. Lincoln: University of Nebraska Press, 1982.
Borowski, Tadeusz. *Tadeusz Borowski: Selected Poems*. Translated by Tadeusz Pióro. Walnut Creek, Calif.: Hit and Run Press, 1990.
Breitwieser, Mitchell. *National Melancholy: Mourning and Opportunity in Classic American Literature*. Stanford: Stanford University Press, 2007.

Bibliography

Brison, Susan. "Outliving Oneself: Trauma, Memory, and Personal Identity." In *Feminists Rethink the Self*, edited by Diana Tietjens Meyers, 12–39. Boulder, Colo.: Westview Press, 1997.

Bross, Kristina. "Dying Saints, Vanishing Savages: 'Dying Indian Speeches' in Colonial New England Literature." *Early American Literature* 36, no. 3 (2001): 325–52.

Browning, Robert. *Robert Browning, Selected Poems*. London: Penguin, 1989.

Burns, Robert. *The Complete Poetical Works of Robert Burns*. Boston: Houghton Mifflin, 1897.

Burt, Olive Wooley, ed. *American Murder Ballads and Their Stories*. New York: Oxford University Press, 1985.

Caruth, Cathy. *Unclaimed Experience: Trauma, Narrative, and History*. Baltimore: Johns Hopkins University Press, 1996.

Cavitch, Max. *American Elegy: The Poetry of Mourning from the Puritans to Whitman*. Minneapolis: University of Minnesota Press, 2007.

Celan, Paul. *Selected Prose and Poems of Paul Celan*. Translated by John Felstiner. New York: W. W. Norton, 2001.

Chase, Cynthia. "Reading Epitaphs." In *Deconstruction Is/in America: A New Sense of the Political*, edited by Anselm Haverkamp, 52–59. New York: New York University Press, 1995.

Cheever, George B., ed. *The American Common-place Book of Poetry*. Boston: Carter and Hendee, 1832.

Clark, Tom. *Fractured Karma*. Santa Rosa, Calif.: Black Sparrow Press, 1990.

Cooke, Rose Terry. *Poems*. New York: Peck, 1888.

Crapsey, Adelaide. *The Complete Poems and Collected Letters of Adelaide Crapsey*. Edited by Susan Sutton Smith. Albany: SUNY Press, 1977.

Culler, Jonathan. *The Pursuit of Signs: Semiotics,, Literature, Deconstruction*. Ithaca, N.Y.: Cornell University Press, 1981.

Davison, Peter. *The Poems of Peter Davison, 1957–1995*. New York: Alfred A. Knopf, 1995.

Day-Lewis, C. *The Complete Poems of C. Day-Lewis*. London: Sinclair-Stevenson, 1992.

Day-Lewis, Sean. *C. Day-Lewis: An English Literary Life*. London: Weidenfeld and Nicolson, 1980.

De Man, Paul. "Hypogram and Inscription, Michael Riffaterre's Poetics of Reading." *Diacritics* 11, no. 4 (Winter 1981): 17–35.

———. *The Rhetoric of Romanticism*. New York: Columbia Univesity Press, 1984.

Bibliography

Delbo, Charlotte. *Auschwitz and After*. Translated by Rosette C. Lamont. New Haven: Yale University Press, 1995.

Dennis, Nigel. "Arthur from the Barge: A Study of Last Words." *Encounter* 98 (November 1961): 27–31.

Derrida, Jacques. *The Gift of Death*. Translated by David Wills. Chicago: University of Chicago Press, 1995.

———. *Limited Inc*. Evanston, Ill.: Northwestern University Press, 1988.

———. *Memoires for Paul de Man*. New York: Columbia University Press, 1989.

———. *The Work of Mourning*. Edited by Pascale-Anne Brault and Michael Naas. Chicago: University of Chicago Press, 2001.

Dickinson, Emily. *The Poems of Emily Dickinson*. Edited by R. W. Franklin. 3 vols. Cambridge, Mass.: Belknap Press of Harvard University Press, 1998.

Dollimore, Jonathan. *Death, Desire and Loss in Western Culture*. New York: Routledge, 2001.

Donne, John. *John Donne: The Major Works*. Edited by John Carey. Oxford: Oxford University Press, 1990.

Douglas, Ann. *The Feminization of American Culture*. New York: Farrar, Straus and Giroux, 1977.

Drelincourt, Charles. *The Christian's Consolations against the Fear of Death*. Philadelphia: James Kay, Jun and Brother, 1836.

Dunn, Douglas. *Elegies*. London: Faber and Faber, 1985.

Durrell, Lawrence. *Collected Poems: 1931–1974*. New York: Viking Press, 1980.

Edgette, J. Joseph. "The Epitaph and Personality Revelation." In *Cemeteries and Gravemarkers: Voices of American Culture*, edited by Richard E. Meyer, 87–102. Logan: Utah State University Press, 1992.

Eliot, T. S. *T. S. Eliot: The Complete Poems and Plays, 1909–1950*. New York: Harcourt Brace, 1952.

Farrell, James. *Inventing the American Way of Death, 1830–1920*. Philadelphia: Temple University Press, 1980.

Faust, Drew Gilpin. *This Republic of Suffering: Death and the American Civil War*. New York: Alfred A. Knopf, 2008.

Felman, Shoshana, and Dori Laub. *Testimony: Crises of Witnessing in Literature, Psychoanalysis, and History*. New York: Routledge, 1992.

Flanders, Judith. *Inside the Victorian Home: A Portrait of Domestic Life in Victorian England*. New York: W. W. Norton, 2003.

Forché, Carolyn, ed. *Against Forgetting: Twentieth-Century Poetry of Witness*. New York: W. W. Norton, 1993.

Fraser, G. S. *Poems of G. S Fraser*. Leicester: Leicester University Press, 1981.

Freud, Sigmund. *Thoughts on War and Death*, vol. 14, *The Standard Edition of the Complete Psychological Works of Sigmund Freud*. Edited by James Strachey. 24 vols. London: Hogarth Press, 1915.

———. *Totem and Taboo*, vol. 13, *The Standard Edition of the Complete Psychological Works of Sigmund Freud*. Edited by James Strachey. 24 vols. London: Hogarth Press, 1913.

Fried, Debra. "Repetition, Refrain, and Epitaph." ELH 53, no. 3 (Autumn 1986): 615–32.

Fry, Paul. "The Absent Dead: Wordsworth, Byron, and the Epitaph." *Studies in Romanticism* 17 (1978): 413–33.

Fuller, Roy. *New and Collected Poems, 1934–84*. London: Secker and Warburg, 1985.

Gibb, Robert. *The Origins of Evening*. New York: W. W. Norton, 1988.

Gibson, Scott, ed. *Blood & Tears: Poems for Matthew Shepard*. New York: Painted Leaf Press, 1999.

Gilbert, Sandra M. *Death's Door: Modern Dying and the Ways We Grieve*. New York: W. W. Norton, 2006.

———. *Inventions of Farewell: A Book of Elegies*. New York: W. W. Norton, 2001.

———. *Wrongful Death*. New York: W. W. Norton, 1995.

Gittings, Clare. *Death, Burial and the Individual in Early Modern England*. London: Croom Helm, 1984.

Glück, Louise. *Descending Figure*. New York: Ecco Press, 1980.

Grigson, Geoffrey. *Collected Poems, 1963–1980*. London: Allison and Busby, 1982.

———. *A Skull in Salop and Other Poems*. London: Macmillan, 1967.

Gunn, Thom. *The Man with Night Sweats*. London: Faber and Faber, 1992.

Guthke, Karl S. *Last Words: Variations on a Theme in Cultural History*. Princeton: Princeton University Press, 1992.

H. D. *H. D. Collected Poems, 1912–1944*. Edited by Louis L. Martz. New York: New Directions, 1983.

Hadas, Pamela White. *Designing Women*. New York: Alfred A. Knopf, 1979.

Hall, Donald. *Without*. New York: Houghton Mifflin, 1999.

Hammond, Jeffrey A. *The American Puritan Elegy: A Literary and Cultural Study*. Cambridge: Cambridge University Press, 2000.

Hardy, Thomas. *The Complete Poems of Thomas Hardy*. Edited by James Gibson. London: Macmillan, 1976.

Bibliography

Harper, Frances Ellen Watkins. "Bury Me in a Free Land." *Anti-Slavery Bugle* 20 (November 1858).
Hatto, Arthur T., ed. *Eos: An Enquiry into the Theme of Lovers' Meetings and Partings at Dawn in Poetry*. London: Mouton, 1965.
Here begynneth a lytell treatyse called Ars moriendi. Westminster: Wynken de Worde, 1497.
Hesketh, Pheobe. *The Leave Train: New and Selected Poems*. London: Enitharmon Press, 1994.
Hirsch, Edward. "The Work of Lyric: Night and Day." *Georgia Review* 57, no. 2 (Summer 2003): 368–80.
Holmes, Janet. *The Physicist at the Mall*. Tallahasee, Fla.: Anhinga Press, 1994.
Hughes, Langston. *The Collected Poems of Langston Hughes*. Edited by Arnold Rampersad. New York: Vintage Books, 1994.
Jackson, Helen Hunt. *Poems*. Boston: Roberts Brothers, 1892.
Jacobs, Joseph. "The Dying of Death." *Fortnightly Review* (July–December 1899): 264–69.
Jalland, Pat. *Death in the Victorian Family*. Oxford: Oxford University Press, 1996.
Jarrell, Randall. *The Complete Poems*. New York: Farrar, Straus and Giroux, 1999.
———. *Little Friend, Little Friend*. New York: Dial Press, 1945.
Johnson, Barbara. *Persons and Things*. Cambridge, Mass.: Harvard University Press, 2008.
———. *A World of Difference*. Baltimore: Johns Hopkins University Press, 1987.
Johnson, Greg. *Aid and Comfort*. Gainesville: University of Florida Press, 1993.
Kay, Dennis. *Melodious Tears: The English Funeral Elegy from Spenser to Milton*. Oxford: Oxford University Press, 1990.
Keble, John. *The Christian Year*. London: J. M. Dent and Sons, 1827.
———. *Keble's Lectures on Poetry, 1832–1841*. Translated by Edward Kershaw Francis. 2 vols. Oxford: Clarendon Press, 1912.
Kristeva, Julia. *Powers of Horror: An Essay on Abjection*. New York: Columbia University Press, 1982.
Kselman, Thomas A. *Death and the Afterlife in Modern France*. Princeton: Princeton University Press, 1993.
Lacan, Jacques. *Écrits: The First Complete Edition in English*. Translated by Bruce Fink. New York: W. W. Norton, 2007.

Laderman, Gary. *The Sacred Remains: American Attitudes toward Death, 1799–1883*. New Haven: Yale University Press, 1996.

Langer, Lawrence L. *Art from the Ashes*. New York: Oxford University Press, 1995.

Larkin, Philip. *Collected Poems*. London: Faber and Faber, 2003.

Lee, Hermione. *Virginia Woolf's Nose: Essays on Biography*. Princeton: Princeton University Press, 2005.

Levenson, Michael H. *Geneology of Modernism: A Study of English Literary Doctrine, 1908–1922*. Cambridge: Cambridge University Press, 1984.

Levin, Dana. "The Heroics of Style: A Study in Three Parts." *American Poetry Review* 35, no. 2 (March/April 2006): 45–47.

Lewes, George Henry. *The Life of Goethe*. London: Smith, Elder, and Co., 1864.

Lockyer, Herbert. *Last Words of Saints and Sinners*. Grand Rapids, Mich.: Kregel, 1969.

Lomax, John A., and Alan Lomax. *American Ballads and Folk Ballads*. New York: Macmillan, 1934.

Masters, Edgar Lee. *Spoon River Anthology*. New York: Macmillan, 1915.

Maurice, Priscilla. *Sickness, Its Trials and Blessings, to which is appended Prayers for the Sick and Dying*. New York: Thomas N. Stanford, 1856.

McIntyre, Ian. *Dirt & Diety: A Life of Robert Burns*. London: HarperCollins, 1995.

Merwin, W. S. *The Second Four Books of Poems*. Port Townsend, Wash.: Copper Canyon Press, 1993.

Middlebrook, Diane Wood. *Anne Sexton: A Biography*. Boston: Houghton Mifflin, 1991.

Milford, Nancy. *Savage Beauty: The Life of Edna St. Vincent Millay*. New York: Random House, 2001.

Millay, Edna St. Vincent. *Collected Poems*. Edited by Norma Millay. New York: Harper and Row, 1956.

Millier, Brett C. *Elizabeth Bishop: Life and the Memory of It*. Berkeley: University of California Press, 1993.

Mills-Court, Karen. *Poetry as Epitaph: Representation and Poetic Language*. Baton Rouge: Louisiana State University Press, 1990.

Miranda, Gary. *Listeners at the Breathing Place*. Princeton: Princeton University Press, 1978.

Monette, Paul. *Borrowed Time*. New York: Avon, 1990.

———. *Love Alone: Eighteen Elegies for Rog*. New York: St. Martin's Press, 1988.

Bibliography

Moulton, Louise Chandler. *In the Garden of Dreams: Lyrics and Sonnets*. Boston: Roberts Brothers, 1891.

———. *The Poems and Sonnets of Louise Chandler Moulton*. Boston: Little, Brown, 1909.

Murray, David. *Forked Tongues: Speech, Writing and Representation in North American Indian Texts*. London: Pinter Publishers, 1991.

O'Connor, Mary Catharine. *The Art of Dying Well: The Development of the Ars Moriendi*. New York: Columbia University Press, 1942.

Orr, Gregory. *City of Salt*. Pittsburgh: University of Pittsburgh Press, 1995.

Pagis, Dan. *The Selected Poetry of Dan Pagis*. Translated by Stephen Mitchell. Berkeley: University of California Press, 1996.

Parker, Alan Michael. "Aubade: The Hotel Cleveland." *Paris Review* 39, no. 143 (Summer 1997): 227.

Pastan, Linda. *A Fraction of Darkness*. New York: W. W. Norton, 1985.

Paxson, James J. *The Poetics of Personification*. Cambridge: Cambridge University Press, 1994.

Payne, John. *The Poetical Works of John Payne*. Vol. 2. London: Villon Society, 1902.

———. *The Way of the Winepress*. London: John Payne Society, 1920.

Petrino, Elizabeth A. *Emily Dickinson and Her Contemporaries: Women's Verse in America, 1820–1885*. Hanover: University of New England, 1998.

Phelps, Austin. *The Still Hour: Or, Communion with God*. Boston: Gould and Lincoln, 1860.

Phelps, Elizabeth Stuart. *Songs of the Silent World*. Boston: Houghton Mifflin, 1891.

Phillips, Kate. *Helen Hunt Jackson: A Literary Life*. Berkeley: University of California Press, 2003.

Plath, Sylvia. *The Collected Poems of Sylvia Plath*. Edited by Ted Hughes. New York: HarperPerennial, 1992.

Pound, Ezra. *Lustra of Ezra Pound, with Earlier Poems*. New York: Alfred A. Knopf, 1917.

———. *Make It New: Essays*. London: Faber and Faber, 1934.

Pound, Louise. *American Ballads and Songs*. New York: C. Scribner's Sons, 1922.

Preminger, Alex, and T. V. F. Brogan, eds. *The New Princeton Encyclopedia of Poetry and Poetics*. Princeton: Princeton University Press, 1993.

Quigley, Christine. *The Corpse: A History*. Jefferson, N.C.: McFarland, 1996.

Ramazani, Jahan. *Poetry of Mourning: The Modern Elegy from Hardy to Heaney*. Chicago: University of Chicago Press, 1994.

Ray, David. *Demons in the Diner*. Ashland, Ohio: Ashland Poetry Press, 1999.

Rich, Adrienne. *Collected Early Poems: 1950–1970*. New York: W. W. Norton, 1993.

———. *The Dream of a Common Language*. New York: W. W. Norton, 1978.

Richardson, James. *Interglacial: New and Selected Poems & Aphorisms*. Keene, N.Y.: Ausable, 2004.

Richardson, Ruth. *Death, Dissection, and the Destitute*. 2nd ed. Chicago: University of Chicago Press, 2000.

Riffaterre, Michael. "Prosopopeia." *Yale French Studies* 69 (1985): 107–23.

Rilke, Rainer Maria. *In Praise of Mortality: Duino Elegies and Sonnets to Orpheus*. Translated by Anita Barrows and Joanna Macy. New York: Riverhead Books, 2005.

Robertson, James. *Poems on Several Occasions*. 2nd ed. London: T. Davies, G. Robinson, T. Cadell, and T. Slack, 1780.

Roethke, Theodore. *The Collected Poems of Theodore Roethke*. Garden City, N.Y.: Doubleday, 1966.

Romero, Lora. *Home Fronts: Domesticity and Its Critics in the Antebellum United States*. Durham: Duke University Press, 1997.

Ruby, Jay. *Secure the Shadow: Death and Photography in America*. Cambridge, Mass.: MIT Press, 1995.

Sacks, Peter. *The English Elegy: Studies in the Genre from Spenser to Yeats*. Baltimore: Johns Hopkins University Press, 1985.

Samaras, Nicholas. *Hands of the Saddlemaker*. New Haven: Yale University Press, 1992.

Saville, Jonathan. *The Medieval Erotic Alba: Structure as Meaning*. New York: Columbia University Press, 1972.

Schiff, Hilda, ed. *Holocaust Poetry*. New York: St. Martin's Griffin, 1995.

Scholes, Robert. *Semiotics and Interpretation*. New Haven: Yale University Press, 1982.

Scodel, Joshua. *The English Poetic Epitaph: Commemoration and Conflict from Jonson to Wordsworth*. Ithaca, N.Y.: Cornell University Press, 1991.

Seeman, Erik. *Pious Persuasions: Laity and Clergy in Eighteenth-Century New England*. Baltimore: Johns Hopkins University Press, 1999.

———. "Reading Indians' Deathbed Scenes: Ethnohistorical and Rep-

Bibliography

resentational Approaches." *Journal of American History* 88, no. 1 (2001): 17–47.
Sexton, Anne. *The Complete Poems*. Boston: Houghton Mifflin, 1981.
———. *The Death Notebooks*. Boston: Houghton Mifflin, 1974.
Shairp, J. C. Preface to *The Christian Year*, by John Keble, vii–xxiv. London: J. M. Dent and Sons, 1827.
Shapiro, Harvey. *Selected Poems*. Manchester U.K.: Carcanet, 1997.
Shapiro, Karl Jay. *Collected Poems, 1940–1978*. New York: Random House, 1978.
Sigal, Gale. *Erotic Dawn-Song of the Middle Ages: Voicing the Lyric Lady*. Gainesville: University Press of Florida, 1996.
Sigourney, Lydia. *The Faded Hour*. New York: Robert Carter and Brothers, 1853.
———. *Letters of Life*. New York: D. Appleton, 1866.
———. *Letters to Young Ladies*. Hartford, Conn.: P. Canfield, 1833.
———. *Pocahontas, and Other Poems*. New York: Harper and Brothers, 1841.
———. *The Weeping Willow*. Hartford: Henry S. Parsons, 1847.
Sloane, David Charles. *The Last Great Necessity: Cemeteries in American History*. Baltimore: Johns Hopkins University Press, 1991.
Smith, Barbara Herrnstein. *Poetic Closure: A Study of How Poems End*. Chicago: University of Chicago Press, 1968.
Smith, D. Vance. *Arts of Dying*. Unpublished manuscript, n.d.
Smith, Stevie. *Collected Poems*. New York: New Directions, 1976.
Spargo, R. Clifton. *The Ethics of Mourning: Grief and Responsibility in Elegiac Literature*. Baltimore: Johns Hopkins University Press, 2004.
Spofford, Harriet Prescott. Introduction to *The Poems and Sonnets of Louise Chandler Moulton*, by Louise Chandler Moulton, v–xix. Boston: Little, Brown, 1909.
Stevenson, Anne. *Bitter Fame: A Life of Sylvia Plath*. Boston: Houghton Mifflin, 1989.
Swinburne, Algernon Charles. *Poems and Ballads*. London: Chatto and Windus, 1897.
Tennyson, Alfred Lord. *Tennyson's Poetry*. Edited by Robert W. Hill. New York: W. W. Norton, 1971.
Tennyson, Hallam. *Alfred Lord Tennyson: A Memoir*. Vol. 1. New York: Macmillan, 1897.
Thomas, Dylan. *The Poems of Dylan Thomas*. Edited by Daniel Jones. New York: New Directions, 1971.

Tileston, Mary Wilder Foote, ed. *Sursum Corda: Hymns for the Sick and Suffering*. Boston: Roberts Brothers, 1877.

Vendler, Helen. *Invisible Listeners: Lyric Intimacy in Herbert, Whitman, and Ashbery*. Princeton: Princeton University Press, 2005.

Verdery, Katherine. *The Political Lives of Dead Bodies: Reburial and Postsocialist Change*. New York: Columbia University Press, 1999.

Vickery, John B. *The Modern Elegiac Temper*. Baton Rouge: Louisiana State University Press, 2006.

Werner, Martin. *The Formation of Christian Dogma*. London: A. and C. Black, 1957.

Westwood, Thomas. *Poems*. London: H. Hughes, 1840.

Wheeler, Michael. *Death and the Future Life in Victorian Literature and Theology*. Cambridge: Cambridge University Press, 1990.

White, Helen C. *English Devotional Literature [Prose], 1600–1640*. Madison: University of Wisconsin Press, 1931.

Whitman, Walt. *Leaves of Grass and Other Writings*. Edited by Michael Moon. New York: W. W. Norton, 2002.

Wilbur, Richard. *Collected Poems, 1943–2004*. Orlando, Fla.: Harcourt, 2004.

Williams, William Carlos. *The Collected Poems of William Carlos Williams*. Vol. 1. Edited by A. Walton Litz and Christopher MacGowan. New York: New Directions, 1986.

Wolfson, Susan J., and Peter J. Manning, eds. *Selected Poems of Hood, Praed and Beddoes*. London: Penguin, 2000.

Wolosky, Shira, ed. *Major Voices: 19th Century American Women's Poetry*. New Milford, Conn.: Toby Press, 2003.

Wordsworth, William. *Essays upon Epitaphs*. Vol. 2. Edited by W. J. B. Owen and Jane Worthington Smyser. London: Oxford University Press, 1974.

Worley, Jeff. "Sunday Aubade." *Literary Review* 39, no. 1 (Fall 1995): 38–39.

Yacovone, Donald. "Sacred Land Regained: Frances Ellen Watkins Harper and 'The Massachusetts Fifty-Fourth,' a Lost Poem." *Pennsylvania History* 62, no. 1 (Winter 1995): 90–110.

Yeats, W. B. *The Collected Poems of W. B. Yeats*. Edited by Richard J. Finneran. New York: Scribner, 1996.

Zeiger, Melissa F. *Beyond Consolation: Death, Sexuality, and the Changing Shapes of Elegy*. Ithaca, N.Y.: Cornell University Press, 1997.

Index

abandonment, fear of, 49, 82–86, 101
Abel, 72
Achilles, 93
African Americans, 17, 117n120
afterlife, 69
Agamben, Giorgio, 74
agency of the deceased, 18, 33, 60, 69, 76
"Ah, Are you Digging on my Grave?" (Hardy), 48
AIDS poems, 31–33, 35, 120n51
"Alba" (Pound), 92–93
American Commonplace Book of Poetry, The (Cheever), 13
American murder ballads, 20–22
Anatomy Act (1832), 47, 123n8
animation of the poet, 77
anti-aubades, 95
Antler, 37
apocryphal last words, 38–39
apostrophe, 67–68, 102–3, 105
Ariès, Philippe, 1
ars essendi morti, 45
ars moriendi: corpse poems as, 45; as deathbed manuals, 32; intercessory prayer, and, 13; last-word poems as, 2; as spiritual guides, 114–15n3, 120n49, 120n58; unintentional last words and, 26–31
"Aubade" (Crapsey), 95–97

"Aubade" (Larkin), 99–100
"Aubade" (Stevie Smith), 87–88
"Aubade and Elegy" (Bishop), 103–5, 129n39
aubades: about, 78–82, 126–27n7; commuter, 93–94; compared to elegies, 101–6; dialogues in, 83–89; lovers, abandonment by, 82–86, 101; lovers departing, 90–95; lovers refusing to depart, 95–98; motherhood and, 128n22; preview of cadavers, 92–93; revival and survival, 102–6; single-lover aubades, 98–101; waiting and loss, 83–89
audience, 5, 14–15
Augustine, 74
Auschwitz and After (Delbo), 65
automobiles, 93–94
Awful Rowing Towards God, The (Sexton), 40

Babii Yar, 65
"Ballads of Lenin" (Hughes), 58
banality of death, 24–30, 121n67
"Barren Women" (Plath), 128n22
Barthes, Roland: "The Death of the Author," 74; Derrida on, 41; *Fragments d'un discours amoureux*, 82–86; on love, 90–91, 97; parental abandonment, 101–2

Index

Bashō, 84
Beaty, Nancy Lee, 116n11
"Because I could not stop for Death" (Dickinson), 53
"Before Parting" (Swinburne), 91–92
bereavement and the bereaved, 10–12, 19–20, 72–73. *See also* ars moriendi; consolation poetry; mourning; witnessing
"Between the World and Me" (Wright), 59–61
Beyond the Pleasure Principle (Freud), 86
biblical figures, 72, 93
Bishop, Elizabeth, 71–73, 103–5, 126n1, 128–29n37, 129n39
Blanchot, Maurice, 41
Borowski, Tadeusz, 64
"Bring me the sunset in a cup" (Dickinson), 51
Brison, Susan, 124n30
Browning, Robert, 90–91
Burns, Robert, 23, 39, 121n66
"Bury Me in a Free Land" (Watkins), 17, 117n120

cadavers: commodification of, 46–50; depersonalization of, 63–65, 124n23; dissection, 47, 123n8; grave robbing, 47; modern warfare and genocide, 62–67; preview of, in aubades, 92–93; suitability of corpse poems for, 73–77
cancer poems, 33–35
Catholicism, 115n5
Cavitch, Max, 114n7
Celan, Paul, 64, 75
chansons, 79
Christian good death, 10–11, 13, 24, 27, 31–33, 114–15nn2–3

Christianity. *See* Catholicism; Evangelical literature; Protestantism
Christian Scientists, 30
Christian's Consolations against the Fear of Death, The (Drelincourt), 114–15n3, 120n58
Christian Year, The (Keble), 11
citationality, 40–41, 125n36
Clark, Tom, 40
closure and defiance of death, 42–43
comic corpse poems, 46–50
Communist Party, 58
commuter aubades, 93–94
condemnation, 21
consolation poetry, 4–5, 11–20, 107–9, 113n3
"Consolation Prayer for a Dying Minister" (Drelincourt), 120n58
Cooke, Rose Terry, 21–22
corpse poems: about, 44–46; all literature as, 77; ars moriendi as, 45; comic, 46–50; compared to elegies, 67–73, 125n42; historical memory of, 61–67; history of, 122n4; as means of reaffirming death, 71–73; political, 57–61; religious, 50–57; suitability of, 73–77; survival and, 124n30. *See also* prosopopoeia
Crane, Hart, 40
Crapsey, Adelaide, 95–97
"Cruel Brother, The" (ballad), 21
cultural figures, 72
curses, 21

Danton, Georges, 66
Davison, Peter, 70
dawn, imagery of, 87–89, 93
dawn songs: abandonment of

Index

lovers, 82–86; about, 78–86; departing lover, 90–95; lovers refusing to leave, 95–98; revival and survival, 102–6; single-lover aubades, 98–101; waiting and loss, 83–89. *See also* aubades

Day-Lewis, C., 9, 39

Day-Lewis, Sean, 39, 121n67

death: animation of the poet, 77; Christian good, 10–11, 13, 24, 27, 31–33, 114–15nn2–3; closure, 42–43; commodification of the cadaver, 46–50; contentment of the deceased, 71; deathbed manuals and preparation for, 32; dehumanizing and bureaucratization of, 1, 4–5, 24–25, 118–19n38, 124n23; demystification or idealization of, 28–30, 55–57; denial of, 122n3; fear of, 1–2, 46; language and, 46, 75; secrets of, 18–20; shameful, 30; social history of, 124n23; space between life and, 50–57; spiritual guides for, 13–14, 114–15n3, 120n49, 120n58

"Death and Dying Words of Poor Mailie . . . , The" (Burns), 23

deathbed manuals, 32, 114–15n3

"Death of the Author, The" (Barthes), 74

"Death of the Ball Turret Gunner, The" (Jarrell), 62–63

Death's Door (Gilbert), 118n37

"Death thou shalt die" (Donne), 50

defascination, 92

defiance, 20–24, 42–43

deflation poems, 57–58

dehumanizing and bureaucratization of death, 1, 4–5, 24–25, 118–19n38, 124n23

Delbo, Charlotte, 65

de Man, Paul, 68, 125n36

demystification or idealization of death, 28–30, 55–57

departing lover aubades, 90–98

Derrida, Jacques, 40–41, 74, 120n52

Desdemona complex, 22, 118n30

De Trinitate (Augustine), 74

dialogues in aubades, 83–89

Dickinson, Emily: on afterlife, 69; corpse poems of, 44, 50–53, 56–57, 123n11, 123n13; as deathbed witness, 117n122; on "dying eye," 116n9; "I heard a Fly buzz - when I died," 18; "The last Night that She lived," 18–19; on poetry and death, 74–75

dissection, 47, 123n8

Dollimore, Jonathan, 122n76

Donne, John, 50

"Do Not Go Gentle into that Good Night" (Thomas), 118n36

"Do People moulder equally" (Dickinson), 50

Douglas, Ann, 39

Drelincourt, Charles, 114–15n3, 120n58

Dunn, Douglas, 33–34

"Dying of Death, The" (Jacobs), 57

dying voice, 2

"Edge" (Plath), 40

elegies: aubades as, 78–83; compared to aubades, 101–6; compared to corpse poems, 67–73, 125n42; definition of, 6, 127n9; ethics of, 4–8, 107–11; format of, 9; and loss, 113n5; as survival medium, 78

143

Elegies (Dunn), 33–34
"Elegy" (Merwin), 8, 107, 109
Eliot, T. S., 61, 124n24
End of the Poem, The (Agamben), 74
Eos, 93
"Epitaph" (Grigson), 55–56
eros, 86–87, 102, 106
ethics, 4–8, 41, 107–11, 113n3
Ethics of Mourning, The (Spargo), 113n3
Eurydice, 70–71
"Eurydice" (H.D.), 70–71
"Eurydice" (Hadas), 70
"Eurydice in Darkness" (Davison), 70
Evangelical literature, 10–11, 13, 31–33
Eve, 93
execution broadsides, 20
existence, fear of, 98–101

"Faithful" (Cooke), 21–22
"Farewell to Maria" (Borowski), 64
fear: of abandonment, 49, 82–86, 101; of death, 1–2, 46; of existence, 98–101
fictional voice. *See* corpse poems
Flanders, Judith, 119n43
flowers, symbolism of, 93–94, 127n11
folk ballads, 20–23, 42–43, 49
forbidden love, 78–82
forgiveness, 21–22
Foucault, Michel, 122n3
Fragments d'un discours amoureux (Barthes), 82–86
Freud, Sigmund, 49, 86, 99–100
"Front, A" (Jarrell), 109–11
Fuller, Roy, 69

Geiger, Melissa, 33
gender, 16, 21–22, 116n15. *See also* women
genocide, 62–67, 75
"Ghost Voice" (Fuller), 69
Gibb, Robert, 100–102
Gift of Death, The (Derrida), 120n52
Gilbert, Sandra, 24–25, 118n37
Glatstein, Jacob, 65
Goethe, Johann Wolfgang von, 37, 121n75
good death, 114–15nn2–3
"Grave my little cottage is, The" (Dickinson), 52
grave robbing, 47
"Green Room, The" (Sexton), 40
Grigson, Geoffrey, 55–56
Gunn, Thom, 32
Guthke, Karl S., 118n30

Hadas, Pamela White, 70
Hall, Donald, 33–34
Hallam, Arthur, 7
Hardy, Thomas, 44, 48, 69
Harper, Frances Ellen Watkins, 17
H.D., 44, 70–71
"Heavy Women" (Plath), 128n22
Herrick, Robert, 122n4
Hirsch, Edward, 126n5
historical memory, 61–67
Holocaust poems, 64–65, 124n27
Hood, Thomas, 47–48, 51
horizontal form of address, 14–15
Horwitz, Roger, 33, 120n51
Hughes, Langston, 58

"I am alive – I guess" (Dickinson), 53
Icarus, 72
"I heard a Fly buzz – when I died" (Dickinson), 18

Index

immortality, 36, 38, 75, 99–100
In Memoriam (Tennyson), 7
intercessory prayer, 13
Interglacial (Richardson), 43
"Interim" (Millay), 26–28
"In the Village" (Bishop), 126n1

Jackson, Helen Hunt, 15–16, 116–17n16
Jacobs, Joseph, 57
Jalland, Pat, 10, 115–16n7
Jarrell, Randall, 44, 62–64, 109–11
"Jealous Lover, The" (ballad), 21
"Johnny Randall" (ballad), 21
Johnson, Barbara, 7
Johnson, Greg, 32
Jonson, Ben, 51, 122n4
Judgment Day, 50

Keats, John, 126–27n7
Keble, John, 11, 115–16n7
Kenyon, Jane, 34
Kristeva, Julia, 61
Kumin, Maxine, 40

"La Belle Dame Sans Merci" (Keats), 126–27n7
"Lament" (Gunn), 32
language and death, 46, 75
Larkin, Philip, 99–100
"Last Good-by, The" (Moulton), 25–26
lastness, power of, 35–43
"last Night that She lived, The" (Dickinson), 18–19
last rites, 115n5
"last Speech and Dying Words of Willy . . . , The" (Robertson), 23
last words, 26–31, 38–39, 115n5
"Last Words" (Antler), 37
"Last Words" (Day-Lewis), 9
"Last Words" (Jackson), 15–16

"Last Words" (Westwood), 14
"Last Words of Hart Crane as He Becomes One with the Gulf" (Clark), 40
"Last Words of an Indian Chief" (Sigourney), 16
"Last Words of My English Grandmother, The" (Williams), 28–30, 119n45
"Late Aubade, A." (Wilbur), 96–98, 102
Lazarus, 72
Lenin, 58
Letters of Life (Sigourney), 39
Levenson, Michael H., 124n24
Levin, Dana, 35
literary corpse poems, 67–73
loss, 6–7, 83–89, 113n5
"Losses" (Jarrell), 63–64
Love Alone (Monette), 120n51
love and lovers: abandonment of, 82–86; departing, 90–95; forbidden, 78–82; refusing to depart, 95–98; sexual passion, 89–91; single-lover aubades, 98–101; surviving lovers, 102–6
Lover's Discourse, A: Fragments (Barthes), 82–86
Lowell, Robert, 35
lynching, 59–61
lyric poetry, 3, 14, 43, 77, 85, 106. *See also* aubades

"Make me a picture of the sun" (Dickinson), 51
Mallarmé, Stéphane, 41
Margaret and Henrietta (Sigourney), 39
"Mary's Ghost" (Hood), 47–48, 122–23n6
Maud (Tennyson), 53–55
Maurice, Priscilla, 11, 115n6

145

Index

"Meeting at Night" (Browning), 90–91
melancholic mourning, 5, 113n3
Memnon, 93
Merwin, W. S., 8, 107, 109
meter, 16, 29, 80, 126n4
Millay, Edna St. Vincent, 26–28, 39–40
Molofsky, Shirr, 17
Monette, Paul, 32–33, 120n51
moralizing tales, 23
morning and mourning, 78, 85, 87–89, 93, 106, 126n1. *See also* dawn songs
"Morning Song" (Plath), 128n22
motherhood, 128n22
Moulton, Louise Chandler, 25–26, 119n41
mourning: of and by the deceased, 52; excessive, 69; melancholic, 113n3; morning and, 78, 85, 87–89, 93, 106, 126n1. *See also* aubades; bereavement and the bereaved
murder ballads, 20–22
mythological figures, 70–72, 83, 88, 93

Native Americans, 16–17
newness of secular last-word poems, 31–35
"No Goodbyes" (Monette), 33
Nyx, 88

O'Connor, Mary Catharine, 120n49
Odysseus, 83
"On Himselfe" (Herrick), 122n4
"Opening to Satan, An" (Pagis), 66
Orpheus, 70
Orr, Gregory, 94
Ovid, 41

Pagis, Dan, 44, 66
parataxis, 91
parental abandonment, 83, 101–2
parodies of last-word poems, 23–24
"Parting, The" (Rich), 25
"Parting" (Yeats), 87, 89
"Parting at Morning" (Browning), 90–91
Payne, John, 34–35, 99
Penelope, 83
Persephone, 72
Plath, Sylvia, 40, 41, 75–76, 128n22
poetry, 10–12, 74–75, 77. *See also specific types of poems*
political corpse poems, 57–61
Political Lives of Dead Bodies (Verdery), 57
postmodernism, 49–50
Pound, Ezra, 35, 92–93, 102
Pound, Louise, 20, 117n24
prayer, purpose of, 13
Prayers for the Sick and Dying (Maurice), 11
prosopopoeia, 68–70, 103, 125n36. *See also* corpse poems
Protestantism, 10, 50, 115n5. *See also* Christian good death; Evangelical literature
"Psalm" (Celan), 64
purgatory, 50

Ramazani, Jahan, 113n3, 118–19n38
Ray, David, 38
realism, 102
redemption poems, 57–60
religious corpse poems, 50–57
"Resurrection" (Payne), 34–35
retribution, 21
revival and survival, 102–6

Index

reviving voice, 2
rhyme and rhythm, 11
Rich, Adrienne, 25
Richardson, James, 43
Richardson, Ruth, 123n8
Rilke, Rainer Maria, 37
Robertson, James, 23
Roethke, Theodore, 121n75
Romero, Lora, 114n2
Rosen, Ted, 32

Samaras, Nicholas, 94, 102
Samson, 94
"Sandy Burial, A" (Grigson), 55
satirical poems and last word, 23–24
Saville, Jonathan, 81
Schoenberg, Arnold, 97
Scodel, Joshua, 122n4
"Seasons of Prayer" (Ware), 13
secrets of death, 18–20
Seeman, Erik, 116n15
Sexton, Anne, 37–38, 40
sexual passion, 89–91, 95–97
shameful death, 30
Shapiro, Harvey, 95
Shapiro, Karl, 93
Sharp, J. C., 115–16n7
Shatayev, Elvira, 72
Shepard, Matthew, 72
"Signature Event Context" (Derrida), 74
Sigourney, Andrew, 115n6
Sigourney, Lydia, 11, 16, 39
single-lover aubades, 98–101
slavery, 17, 117n120
Smith, Barbara Herrnstein, 122n76
Smith, Stevie, 87–88, 93
Soares, Lota de Macedo, 103–5, 128–29n37, 129n39
social injustices, 58

social relationships, 14–17
Space of Literature, The (Blanchot), 41
Spargo, R. Clifton, 7, 113n3
spiritual guides, 13–14, 114–15n3, 120n49, 120n58
Spofford, Harriet Prescott, 119n41
"Stillborn" (Plath), 75–76
Stowe, Harriet Beecher, 114n2
suburbia, 93–94
"Sunday Aubade" (Worley), 95
Sursum Corda (Tileston), 11, 115n6
surviving lover poems, 102–6. See also dawn songs
surviving voice, 2, 78, 102–6, 124n30
Swinburne, A. C., 91–92

Tennyson, Alfred Lord, 7, 53–55
thanatos, 106
"Thirteen Steps and the Thirteenth of March" (Dunn), 34
Thomas, Dylan, 118n36
Tileston, Mary, 11, 115n6
"To die – without the Dying" (Dickinson), 56–57

Uncle Tom's Cabin (Stowe), 114n2
unintentional last words, 26–31

ventriloquism, 5, 13, 17, 40, 83–89, 110. See also corpse poems; prosopopoeia
Verdery, Katherine, 57
vertical form of address, 14–15
Vickery, John B., 113n5
victims, honoring of, 59–61
Victorian attitudes, 10
Virgin Mary, 93
voice: agency of the deceased, 18, 33, 60, 69, 76; dispassionate nature of, 63; in last-word poems, 2; surviving, 2, 78,

Index

voice (*continued*)
   102–6, 124n30. *See also* corpse poems; prosopopoeia; ventriloquism

waiting and loss, 6–7, 83–89, 113n5
war, modern, 62–67, 86
Ware, Henry, 13
Waste Land, The (Eliot), 62, 124n24
Welcome, Emily Dickinson, 30
Westwood, Thomas, 14
Wheeler, Michael, 114n2, 115–16n7
"Wicked Polly" (ballad), 22–23
Wilbur, Richard, 96–98, 102
Williams, William Carlos, 28–30, 42–43, 119n45
Without (Hall), 33–34

witnessing, 115n6, 116n11, 117n122
women: as abandoned lover, 82–83; consolation poems of, 16; deathbed scenes of, 34; as deathbed witnesses, 115n6; in Dickinson's corpse poems, 51; last words of, 116n15; motherhood, 128n22; murder ballads, 21–22; sorrow of, 93
Wordsworth, William, 51, 68–69
World War I and II, poems of, 62–67, 86
Worley, Jeff, 95
Wright, Richard, 44, 59–61
Wrongful Death (Gilbert), 118n37

Yacovone, Donald, 117n120
Yeats, W. B., 87, 89
Yevtushenko, Yevgeny, 65

Copyright Acknowledgments

All poems by Emily Dickinson reprinted by permission of the publishers and the Trustees of Amherst College from *The Poems of Emily Dickinson*, Thomas H. Johnson, ed., Cambridge, Mass.: The Belknap Press of Harvard University Press, Copyright © 1951, 1955, 1979 by the President and Fellows of Harvard College.

"Aphorism 149," by James Richardson, from *Interglacial: New and Selected Poems & Aphorisms*. Copyright © 2004 by James Richardson. Reprinted with permission of the Permissions Company, Inc., on behalf of Copper Canyon Press, www.coppercanyonpress.org.

"Aubade," by Adelaide Crapsey, reprinted by permission from *Complete Poems and Collected Letters of Adelaide Crapsey* by Susan S. Smith, the State University of New York Press © 1977, State University of New York. All rights reserved.

"Aubade," by Philip Larkin, from *Collected Poems*. Reprinted by permission of Faber and Faber Ltd.

"Aubade," by Stevie Smith, from *Collected Poems of Stevie Smith*, copyright © 1966 by Stevie Smith. Reprinted by permission of New Directions Publishing Corp. Reprinted by permission of Estate of James MacGibbon.

"Aubade and Elegy," by Elizabeth Bishop, from *Edgar Allan Poe & The Juke-Box*, edited and annotated by Alice Quinn. Copyright © 2006 by Alice Helen Methfessel. Reprinted by permission of Farrar, Straus and Giroux, LLC. Reprinted by permission of Carcanet Press Limited.

"The Death of the Ball Turret Gunner" and excerpt from "A Front," by Randall Jarrell, from *The Complete Poems* by Randall Jarrell. Copyright © 1969, renewed 1997 by Mary von S. Jarrell. Reprinted by permission of Farrar, Straus and Giroux, LLC. Reprinted by permission of Faber and Faber Ltd.

Copyright Acknowledgments

"Elegy," by W. S. Merwin, from *The Second Four Books of Poems* by W. S. Merwin. Copyright © 1992 by W. S. Merwin, used by permission of the Wylie Agency LLC.

"Epitaph," by Geoffrey Grigson, from *Collected Poems, 1963–1980*, published by Allison & Busby; and "A Sandy Burial," by Geoffrey Grigson, from *A Skull in Salop and Other Poems*, published by Macmillan. Reprinted by permission of David Higham.

"The Last Words of My English Grandmother," by William Carlos Williams, from *The Collected Poems: Volume I, 1909–1939*, copyright © 1938 by New Directions Publishing Corp. Reprinted by permission of New Directions Publishing Corp. Reprinted by permission of Carcanet Press Limited.

"A Late Aubade," by Richard Wilbur, from *Collected Poems, 1943–2004*, by Richard Wilbur. Copyright © 2004 by Richard Wilbur. Reprinted by permission of Houghton Mifflin Harcourt Publishing Company. All rights reserved.

"An Opening to Satan," by Dan Pagis, from *The Selected Poetry of Dan Pagis*. Reprinted by permission of University of California Press.

"Parting," by W. B. Yeats. Reprinted with the permission of Scribner, a Division of Simon & Schuster, Inc., from *The Collected Works of W. B. Yeats, Volume I: The Poems, Revised*, by W. B. Yeats, edited by Richard J. Finneran. Copyright © 1933 by the Macmillan Company, renewed 1961 by Bertha Georgie Yeats. All rights reserved.

"Stillborn," by Sylvia Plath, from *The Collected Poems of Sylvia Plath*, edited by Ted Hughes. Copyright © 1960, 1965, 1971, 1981 by the Estate of Sylvia Plath. Editorial mat'l copyright © 1981 by Ted Hughes. Reprinted by permission of HarperCollins Publishers. Reprinted by permission of Faber and Faber Ltd.